Tsunami

Iain Macwhirter

FREIGHT
BOOKS

First published 2015

Freight Books
49–53 Virginia Street
Glasgow, G1 1TS
www.freightbooks.co.uk

A CIP catalogue reference for this book is available from the British
Library.

ISBN 978-1-910449-63-9

Typeset by Freight in Plantin
Printed and bound by Bell and Bain, Glasgow

the publisher acknowledges investment from
Creative Scotland toward the publication of this book

Introduction

Tsunami, earthquake, landslide, extinction-level event – the Scottish political world was bereft of superlatives to describe the 2015 General Election that swept away the Scottish Labour Party. It was the most serious electoral upset in Scotland since at least 1931 and has drawn comparisons with the 1918 Sinn Fein landslide in Ireland, though the circumstances are very different. This election drew a line under Labour's half-century-long dominance of Scottish politics. But it did much more than that. The 2015 General Election raised the United Kingdom's constitutional crisis to an altogether higher level. The 56 SNP MPs sitting in Westminster as the third largest UK party poses the Scottish question in a form which the UK political establishment can no longer ignore.

Only twenty years ago, a result like this would have been regarded by the SNP, and probably by Westminster, as a mandate for independence. It is not. Scotland voted to remain within the UK in the independence referendum of 2014. As the First Minister Nicola Sturgeon made clear, even if the SNP had won all 59 Scottish seats it would not have been justification for another referendum. However, it is the clearest demonstration that the constitution of the United Kingdom must change and must do so without delay. It would seem that only the most radical form of home rule, often called devo max, within a new federal United Kingdom, could conceivably now satisfy Scottish demands for autonomy and prevent Scotland taking the final step towards independence. There seems very little prospect of Westminster reforming itself in time.

In *Road to Referendum* (Cargo, 2013/2014), I explained how formal political independence is a very novel aspiration in Scotland, which had remained a relatively content partner in the Union really until the 1990s. In *Disunited Kingdom:*

How Westminster Won a Referendum but Lost Scotland (Cargo, 2014), I explored how the experience of the 2014 referendum campaign, with its unprecedented levels of political engagement, transformed Scotland's attitude to the UK. In this book I ask whether the events of 2014/15 constitute a revolutionary challenge to the established political order which will lead to the end of the Union.

It was the BBC's political presenter and author Andrew Marr who first noted during the 2015 General Election campaign that Scotland appeared to be going through something like 'a national revolution'.[1] It seemed a bit of an exaggeration at the time. We don't do revolution here. The word evokes images of violent overthrow; of barricades and broken heads. But I increasingly believe he was right to pose it in revolutionary terms, because this is now a fundamental struggle over the location of political power. Election landslides have consequences, and one is that there is now a conflict of legitimacy between Westminster and Holyrood.

A glance at the new political map of the UK shows that the old politics of class have been replaced by the politics of nation. The Scottish independence movement is similar in content to the left-wing populist movements like Podemos in Spain and Syriza in Greece, but very different in form. The Scottish National Party has occupied the radical space vacated by the mainstream social democratic party, Labour. It has benefited from popular revulsion with austerity economics, voter disengagement from establishment politics, and the new opportunities for ideological discourse and political organisation presented by social media.

But the SNP is not Podemos or Syriza. It is both an insurgency and also an established party of government. Some of its policies on business taxes, law and order, and local taxation could even be described as conservative. In Chapter One, I look at how Nicola Sturgeon managed this contradiction during the general election, and how the spectre of the 'SNP menace' raised by the UK press and the Conservative Party helped unite Scotland electorally behind the nationalist party.

Chapter Two follows one of Scotland's new MPs, Tommy Sheppard, a former assistant secretary of the Scottish Labour Party, as he secured what was one of Labour's safest seats, Edinburgh East, on a swing of 29%. Sheppard does not describe himself as a nationalist in the conventional sense and his political philosophy is an insight into how the new SNP likes to think of itself. I then look at the diverse backgrounds of the rest of the 56 new SNP MPs to try to understand what makes civic nationalism tick in Scotland.

Chapter Three examines the career of the First Minister Nicola Sturgeon, who emerged during the general election as the most popular leader not only in Scotland but, in some opinion polls, the UK. During the campaign she became arguably the most articulate voice of social democracy in Britain. Her call for a 'progressive alliance' of parties in Westminster was somewhat ironic since her party wishes Scotland to leave it. Having achieved near celebrity status since she took over from Alex Salmond, I suggest that her adoption of what she calls 'utilitarian' nationalism marks her out as a fundamentally different kind of nationalist to her predecessor.

Chapter Four examines the performance of Labour's former Scottish leader Jim Murphy. Some said he was the right man on the wrong side of history – a capable politician who did his best. I argue that his opportunist attempts to outflank the SNP on the left were unconvincing and his subsequent lapse into the rhetoric of the defunct Better Together campaign made a significant contribution to the scale of Labour's defeat. However, Jim Murphy's re-adoption of universalism in welfare policies and his 'new Clause Four' which supposedly gives the Scottish party 'total autonomy' in policy could provide the basis for a new Scottish Labour Party.

Following this election defeat there is not necessarily a way back for Labour and it could suffer 'Pasokification', the fate of the Greek social democratic party Pasok, as the SNP colonises the ground on the Scottish centre and centre left. I suggest that to revive its radical soul Labour could look to the tradition of great Scottish Labour figures from the twentieth century like Tom Johnston and Manny Shinwell and reinvent itself as the Independent Labour Party. However, the party appears to be going in the opposite direction and seems content to remain a 'branch office' of UK Labour.

The SNP's success has led to fears about Scotland becoming a one-party state, and while this is unlikely to be the case because the Scottish Parliament is elected on proportional representation, there are obvious risks when one party dominates a nation's politics. All successful governments become an establishment eventually. In Chapter Five I ask why the putative 'Yes Alliance' did not get off the ground in 2015 despite well meaning efforts to create an electoral alternative to the SNP. Organisations like the Radical Independence Campaign, Hope over Fear, Women for Independence, Common Weal, and National Collective arose during the referendum campaign and mostly continue to function as non-party supporters of independence. I assess the prospects for a new left-wing 'Scotdemos' party, if and when the SNP comes to be regarded as the political establishment in Scotland. The Left Project will only work if the various groupings can overcome their proclivity for factionalism and infighting.

In the final chapter I look at what happens next. An early referendum has been rejected by Nicola Sturgeon, to the disappointment of many SNP supporters. I examine whether Scotland has already achieved what some commentators call 'independence in the mind'. This is the idea that a new generation has now taken over Scottish culture and politics and is already behaving as if Scotland were an independent country. However, there must be limits to Scotland's gradualist process of nation-building and it will eventually confront the realities of power in the UK state. Failing a radical constitutional reform of the UK, the Scottish Parliament seems destined to assume full control of matters like economic policy. This is unlikely to be a consensual process.

On the morning of the referendum Alex Salmond was criticised for proclaiming that, despite the victory of the unionist Better Together campaign, Scotland had 'changed, changed utterly'. That quote from the Irish poet W. B. Yeats referred to the transformation of Irish politics after the bloody 1916 Easter Rising. The fact that Scottish nationalism has been entirely peaceful and democratic shouldn't obscure the fact that its objectives are as revolutionary as those of the Irish nationalists in the last century. It is of great credit to Scotland that it has prosecuted the case for independence without resorting to civil disorder, violence, or extra-parliamentary forms of political action. As we enter what may be the most turbulent and unpredictable period of UK politics since the days of Irish home rule, there is no reason why this revolution should not continue to be a peaceful and even joyous one, as we saw during the referendum campaign. No 'terrible beauty' need be born here.

Chapter One:

Tsunami

The election night Green Room at BBC's Pacific Quay HQ in Glasgow didn't look so much like a room as a small cinema with the seats removed. Three large screens, each surrounded by a litter of armchairs, showed the election night programme presented by Glenn Campbell and the BBC's mountainous political editor Brian Taylor. The guests – politicians, academics and journalists – mostly ignored the screens and used their smartphones to keep track of developments. They stood around in partisan bunches munching tapas but mostly avoiding the complimentary wine as they waited to be plucked from the crowd by production assistants dressed in black and taken to the studio to chat.

I had been here most of the night back on the 18th of September 2014 as the results of the Scottish independence referendum were coming in. I remember the misery on the faces of SNP politicians and Yes campaign luminaries like Pat Kane, the musician postmodernist, and Tommy Sheridan, the leader of Hope over Fear. General Election night 2015 was a very different affair. SNP MSPs and political advisers were walking around with huge grins even before the first result was declared. Sheridan was wearing a yellow SNP badge – he's not a member of the party – and taking beaming selfies with attendees. The Liberal Democrat former Deputy First Minister Lord Wallace had his brave face on. Labour politicians came and went like ghosts.

At first, no one believed the BBC's election night exit poll which forecast that the SNP would win all but one of Scotland's 59 seats. SNP contacts were warning me not to take this seriously. Nicola Sturgeon urged her supporters on Twitter: 'don't believe the exit poll, we're not going to do that'. The SNP were worried that a mere landslide of 35 or 40 seats might look like a setback if it didn't match the truly outlandish forecasts of Professor John Curtice's number crunchers. They needn't have worried.

From the moment the first result was declared at 2.15am for Kilmarnock and Loudoun showing an SNP victory on a 25.3% swing from Labour, the temperature of the Green Room rose rapidly. The BBC's variegated guests realised they were about to witness real history. The excitement was palpable. After so long insisting that, nah, the SNP could never, ever, win that many seats, suddenly, they were.

What to say about it? Journalists grasped for appropriate clichés: Labour's Last Stand? A Hammer Blow to the Union? A Constitutional Rubicon? Defcon Fucked for Labour? Was 'tsunami' disrespectful of the victims of the 2004 Asian tidal wave? 'At least Douglas is safe,' said a Labour party researcher. There were early reports that the former Labour Shadow Foreign Secretary Douglas Alexander had scraped home. He hadn't and he fell within minutes. Neither had the leader of the Scottish Labour Party, Jim Murphy, in East Renfrewshire. Then the safest Labour seat in Scotland, Kirkcaldy and Cowdenbeath, fell to the SNP. Until his retiral last year, this had been held by the former Labour Prime Minster Gordon Brown with a majority of 23,000.

The former Labour First Minister Henry McLeish worked the room telling everyone how he'd been expecting this; that Labour's problems go back at least a decade; and that only an autonomous, 'federal' Scottish Labour Party could survive this massacre. The former leader of the Scottish National Party, Gordon Wilson, reminded me that under the old SNP constitution a simple majority of seats in a UK general election would have been regarded as a mandate for independence. This would've been a super mandate. 'The people who abandoned that policy may be wondering now if it was entirely wise to do so,' he said with a mischievous grin. He has never quite come to terms with the SNP's gradualist approach to national liberation.

As the night wore on it became clear that the SNP had indeed won the most remarkable landslide in Scottish electoral history: 56 out of 59 Scottish seats. Only nine months previously the Nationalists had lost the independence referendum by a significant margin of 55% to 45%; now the losers were winning it all. Alex Salmond announced that there hadn't been a general election swing on this scale – 30% – since 1835. But since only about 40,000 people in Scotland had the vote back then it was hardly a relevant comparison.

Certainly, nothing like this has ever happened in modern times. Swings of 34% and 35% are unprecedented in general elections. The swing to the SNP in Willie Bain's Glasgow North East, a seat the opinion pollsters had suggested Labour might hold, reached 39.3% and broke the BBC's swingometer. Perhaps the most extraordinary feature of the night was that the swing appeared to be nationwide and irrespective of party incumbency. The SNP won every seat in Tayside, all six seats in the North East of Scotland, all but one seat in Edinburgh and Fife, and wiped out the LibDems in the Highlands. The SNP had never won a Glasgow seat at a general election before – now every one of them had fallen to the SNP in the 'tsunami', as everyone started calling it. The former SNP Minister Mike Russell tweeted that this wasn't a 'tsunami', it was an 'extinction level event'.

It certainly looked like the end of days for the Scottish Labour Party. The Shadow Foreign Secretary, Douglas Alexander, was defeated by a twenty-year-old student, Mhairi Black, in Paisley, making her the youngest MP since 1667. She said she intended to finish her Politics degree even though she was going to Westminster. Jim Murphy, the former UK Labour Cabinet Minister and current Scottish Labour leader, lost East

Renfrewshire to another SNP neophyte, Kirsten Oswald. This was the seat he had taken from the Tories back in 1997 and turned into one of Labour's safest seats. That term suddenly seemed quaintly archaic.

Mr Murphy made a suitably humble speech but insisted that he would remain leader and that the fight-back would begin the next day. Under normal circumstances this would have sounded absurd since he was no longer an MP or an MSP, but at the time it looked as if there was simply no one left to take over. Other Labour casualties were less gracious. The former MP for Linlithgow, Michael Connarty, announced that the voters of Scotland had been 'duped' by a 'personality cult' supported by the 'forces of darkness'. The discarded Glasgow South West MP Ian Davidson called for Jim Murphy's resignation. He had famously said towards the end of the 2014 referendum campaign that the only thing left for Better Together was to 'bayonet the wounded'. Now he was sticking the knife into his leader's back.

As dawn broke it was clear that the Labour Party in Scotland had suffered its worst election defeat in at least a century, losing 40 of its 41 seats and raising questions about its continued existence as a serious player in Scottish politics. The only Labour MP left standing was Ian Murray in Edinburgh South, and he was something of an outsider because he departed from Labour policy by opposing the renewal of the Trident nuclear defence system. Students of the Left started raising the question of whether the Scottish Labour Party could come back from this defeat, or whether it might suffer what is called 'Pasokification' after the fate of the Greek socialist party Pasok or PSOE.[2] It dominated politics in the 1980s but has been crushed by the radical populist Syriza and won only 5% in the last Greek general election.

Thoughts also turned to who might lead the Scottish National Party contingent in Westminster since of course its leader, the First Minister Nicola Sturgeon, was not standing.

The former First Minister Alex Salmond was returned as expected as MP for Gordon, the seat long held by the Liberal Democrat veteran Malcolm Bruce. But Salmond struck a curiously jarring note when he announced that 'the Scottish lion has roared this morning across the country'.[3] This is not the kind of sentiment that you would hear from his successor, Nicola Sturgeon. Might Alex Salmond become a parliamentary rival leading this group of parliamentary rookies? Most of the victorious SNP MPs avoided crude triumphalism – probably because most of them could hardly believe that they had won. The SNP may have led the opinion polls from day one in this campaign, but few of the candidates ever believed that they could win all but three of Scotland's Westminster seats.

Labour weren't the only casualties of the night. The Scottish Liberal Democrats lost all but one of their MPs and were wiped off the mainland of Scotland. This included UK political stars like the Treasury Secretary Danny Alexander in Inverness, and the former LibDem leader Charles Kennedy in Ross, Skye, and Lochaber (who was to die a month later of an alcohol-related haemorrhage at the age of fifty-five). He had been the youngest MP in Westminster once: in 1983 when he was twenty-three years old. The Liberal Democrats had poured money and resources into trying to save the East Dunbartonshire seat of another former 'young one' Jo Swinson, the former UK equalities minister, but to no avail.

Many Liberal Democrat seats were lost by heart-breakingly large margins. Liberals had dominated the north of Scotland and been influential in Borders politics for over a century. Now their one solitary MP, Alistair Carmichael, held Orkney and Shetland with a majority of only 800-odd votes. And even his future was soon in doubt. The former Scottish Secretary faced legal action over lies he allegedly told about the leaking of the so-called 'Nikileaks' Scottish Office memo during the general election campaign, claiming that Nicola Sturgeon was a secret supporter of David Cameron. The cost of their UK leader Nick Clegg's adventure in government with the Tories had been higher than in the Liberal Democrats' worst nightmares.

The Conservatives were saved from a 1997 style wipeout when David Mundell scraped home in Dumfries with a majority of 798 over the SNP. Alex Salmond may still jeer that there are more giant pandas in Scotland than Tory MPs, but Mr Mundell was now able to say that the panda/MP ratio also applied to Labour and the Liberal Democrats. It began to dawn on everyone that this election result was shaping up to be a constitutional crisis. The unionist parties in Scotland had been virtually obliterated. We'd all been warned by the opinion pollsters that this would happen, but now that it had, no one quite knew what to make of it.

The BBC's political map of Scotland was now entirely Nationalist Yellow except for a splodge of blue in the far south, a pin-prick of red in Edinburgh, and orange in the islands of the far north. Overall the SNP ended the night with 50% of the votes and 95% of the seats, a result which ignited a new debate about the need for electoral reform. The First Past the Post electoral system certainly worked to magnify the scale of the SNP victory. However, that did not in any way diminish the significance of the result. The SNP stacked up the largest proportion of seats – 95% – the biggest pile of votes – 1,454,436 – and the largest electoral swing – 30% – ever won by any single party in Scottish history, or indeed modern UK history.

The largest contingent of MPs the SNP had ever previously returned to Westminster was 11 in October 1974. They'd lost most of them in 1979 when they withdrew support from the collapsing Labour administration of James Callaghan. I got my first job with the BBC in 1979 as a researcher for the abortive devolution referendum of that year, and I had seen first-hand the shattering effect of the loss of those seats on the Nationalist movement. Back then it would have seemed inconceivable that the SNP could ever win such a landslide. Indeed, Gordon Wilson was right: if they had won an election on this scale in the late 70s, negotiations on independence would probably have begun the very next day.

THE SCOTTISH MENACE

The SNP did not however win the balance of power in the UK parliament as many had expected. The 'nightmare on Downing St', as the conservative press called it, was averted. David Cameron won an unexpected victory in the UK as a whole, even as the SNP had swept the board in Scotland. It was only a majority of 12 seats, but given the almost universal expectation that the Tories would have to share power, this seemed almost a landslide of misplaced expectation. It was certainly a workable majority. But surely the real nightmare on Downing St was this: the most right-wing Conservative government since the 1980s had been elected in Westminster, while Scotland had voted massively for a party of the Nationalist Left. A more constitutionally volatile combination could scarcely be imagined.

The two outcomes were not unrelated, of course, though Labour claims that the SNP had 'let the Tories back in' were without foundation. Labour lost in England as well as in Scotland. But the Conservatives had relied on a highly dubious propaganda campaign to achieve their victory. Scottish National Party MPs were presented as an alien force seeking to 'hold England to ransom'. The Conservatives paid for billboards in English marginal constituencies depicting Alex Salmond in a burglar's black turtleneck picking the wallet out of the back pocket of an English voter. 'Don't Let The SNP Grab Your Cash,' it said, in what must have been one of the most irresponsible pieces of election propaganda since the Zinoviev letter. David Cameron had even said that it would be 'illegitimate' for the Labour leader Ed Miliband to take power if he relied on the votes of Scottish National Party MPs.[4] The former Prime Minister, John Major, was wheeled out to warn of the 'clear and present danger' of SNP involvement in the governance of the UK.[5] As hysteria mounted in the dying weeks of the campaign, the Conservative Home Secretary, Theresa May, topped that by claiming that 'a Labour Government propped up by the SNP could be the biggest constitutional crisis since the Abdication'.[6] Quite why she decided to drag the abdication of Edward VIII in 1936 so that he could marry his American lover into the debate was never entirely clear. The statement led to howls of derision from nationalist supporters on social media and a joke hashtag #greatestcrisissincetheabdication was soon trending at number one on the UK Twitter charts. Boris Johnson added his pennyworth claiming that it would be 'Ajockalypse Now' if Labour tried to lead a government with the support of SNP MPs. The Tory-supporting *Daily Mail* called Nicola Sturgeon 'the most dangerous woman in Britain'. The UK tabloid *The Sun* depicted her (in a tartan bikini) as a 'wrecking ball' out to destroy England.

There is a general consensus among opinion pollsters and political correspondents that the SNP scare worked. Many believe that the last minute surge to the Conservatives on the final two days of the campaign, which gave Cameron victory, was almost entirely down to the fear of a Labour-SNP alliance, even though the prospect of a formal coalition had been ruled out by both Ed Miliband and Nicola Sturgeon.[7] Labour's own assessment, according to a report in *The Guardian*, is that it cost them at least 2.5% of the vote.[8] According to the polling organisation ORB, 25% of voters in a sample of over 2000 said the prospect of the SNP being involved in government in Westminster made them less likely to vote for Ed Miliband.[9] But the repeated warnings in the conservative press about the imminence of 'a shabby deal' did the trick. As Martin Shaw put it in *Open Democracy:*

> The Tory warnings had unmistakable echoes of Benjamin Netanyahu's notorious warning that 'the Arabs are coming' which won him a similar surprise victory, but was all the more astonishing since the Scots – unlike Arabs for Israeli Jews – have never been an enemy of the English in modern times.[10]

It was of course quite reasonable for the Conservatives to raise questions about the wisdom of Labour and SNP policies, and even to warn that a coalition might damage the economy. But to suggest that a Labour government would not be democratically legitimate if it relied on SNP votes in the Commons was beyond normal party political rhetoric. It was contrary to parliamentary democracy as well as objectionable to Scottish voters. Senior Conservative sources even briefed the *Times* newspaper that David Cameron might 'sit tight' in Number Ten after the general election if he won the election but lacked a majority in parliament.[11] Yet there was simply no way, short of a coup, that Mr Cameron could have remained in office if the Tory legislative programme in the Queen's Speech had been rejected by a majority of MPs in the House of Commons.

As the former Cabinet Secretary, Lord O'Donnell, made clear along with other constitutional authorities like Professor Vernon Bogdanor, the largest party does not automatically get to be the government in our system.[12] It is the leader who commands a majority in the House of Commons who gets the keys to Number Ten. And the nationality of the votes doesn't matter.

By demonising Nicola Sturgeon, claiming that Scots

were picking English pockets, and suggesting Scotland's elected representatives did not have the right to vote against a Conservative Queen's Speech, David Cameron was not only targeting Labour, he was inadvertently driving a stake through the heart of the Union. If Scottish MPs are not accorded equal status then the Union is no more. This was, as even the former Tory Scottish Secretary Lord Forsyth said, 'a short term and dangerous' game to play for a political party which claimed to want to keep the United Kingdom united.[13] Conservatives in Scotland were horrified at the rhetoric being used. A former Scottish Conservative press spokesman Andy Maciver wrote (only a few days before polling day) that Cameron's approach was 'poisonous for the Union and poisonous for the Scottish Conservative Party'.[14] In an article in *Conservative Home* he went on: 'There is foaming mouth anger amongst those [Scottish Conservatives] to whom I have spoken…if the SNP could create the Tory campaign, according to my erstwhile colleagues, they would have created the one we have seen for the last week.'

In other words, David Cameron was doing the SNP's job for them. The Prime Minister's rhetorical excess not only delivered victory in the south; it almost certainly contributed to the scale of the SNP's landslide in Scotland. The Tories aroused further constitutional controversy during the campaign by proposing to exclude Scottish MPs from key Commons votes, including a new 'English rate of income tax'. Some conspiracy theories believe, indeed, that the Conservatives actively sought a big SNP vote to diminish Labour strength in Westminster. There was talk about how George Osborne had been 'bigging up' Nicola Sturgeon in the spin room after the BBC TV leaders' debate.[15] Some Conservative backbenchers have certainly toyed with the idea of allowing Scotland to depart the Union and leave them in command of the rest of the UK.

But this 'dump Scotland' theory is hardly credible. David Cameron does not wish to go down in history as the Prime

Minister who presided over the break up of Britain. A chaotic disintegration of the United Kingdom could have damaging consequences for the UK's credit rating and its relations with the European Union at a crucial moment when David Cameron is trying to renegotiate Britain's membership. Then there is the question of Trident submarines located on the Clyde near Glasgow. No UK Conservative Prime Minister would wish to lose the 'independent' nuclear deterrent, or indeed Scotland's continuing oil wealth, which contributes significantly to the balance of payments. No, this was a case of the Conservatives allowing irresponsible campaigning themes to run away with them. It was cock up rather than conspiracy. But the result could well be the same: the dissolution of the Union that David Cameron claims he 'loves'.

MURPHY'S LAW

Ed Miliband did not help Labour's cause in Scotland, nor indeed the cause of the Union, by appearing to endorse the SNP scare. On the BBC's Leaders' Question Time on 29th April he said: 'If the price of having a Labour government is a coalition or a deal with the SNP then it is not going to happen... I'm not going to give in to SNP demands around Trident, around the deficit, or anything like that.' The Labour leader thus tacitly endorsed the UK press claim that Nicola Sturgeon was a dangerous left-winger who would leave Scotland defenceless and increase spending. The Labour Shadow Chancellor, Ed Balls, had made clear he intended to eliminate the UK deficit within 5 years and said that this would mean real cuts in non-protected areas of public spending.[16]

Back in Scotland, confusingly, Jim Murphy was claiming that the SNP were closet Conservatives who were planning deep spending cuts in Scotland. The Scottish Labour leader condemned Nicola Sturgeon's policy of full fiscal autonomy as 'full fiscal austerity' and 'austerity max', and said that the SNP planned to cut more than the Tories.[17] He based this charge on the report by the Institute for Fiscal Studies which said that, if Scotland were to raise all its revenue from taxation in Scotland, there would be a £7.6bn deficit in the first year running to £9.7bn by 2020.[18] If the SNP was prepared to contemplate this immense black hole in the Scottish finances, Murphy argued, it would lead to unimaginable cuts in public services in Scotland and/or massive tax increases. This was fiercely contested by the SNP. They rejected the Institute for Fiscal Studies' calculations and said that, anyway, 'Full Fiscal Responsibility' was irrelevant because the big parties would vote against it in Westminster. What was at issue, said Nicola Sturgeon, was the commitment made by Labour to abolish the deficit within one UK parliament.

Labour were of course fully entitled to challenge the SNP's policy on FFA – which was after all in their manifesto – but the problem was the coherence of the Labour message. It made little sense for them to claim that 'a vote for the SNP is a vote for the Conservatives' when the Tories and their supportive newspapers were portraying the SNP as a party of the far left. Even Ed Miliband was saying the SNP's spending plans were dangerously expansionary.[19]

UK newspapers were full of claims that Nicola Sturgeon would wreck the UK by launching an irresponsible £180bn spending boom – a reference to the First Minister's speech to University College London in February in which she proposed to increase spending on investment by 0.5% of GDP each year.[20] She was being cast as the 'Red Queen', taking 'a wrecking ball' to the UK economy. Yet, the main thrust of the Labour campaign in Scotland was that the SNP were 'the Tories' little helpers' and that 'every vote for the SNP is a vote for David Cameron'. This created a dissonance which the SNP exploited by insisting that Labour didn't know what it stood for.

Why did Labour go down this road? Well, Scottish Labour politicians have long believed that the SNP's progressive postures are phoney. They have convinced themselves that the SNP are not really social democrats at all, but political con-artists. As Stephen Daisley, the STV digital political editor, put it: '[The SNP] have secured the support of much of the Scottish Left without once venturing beyond the low-tax, pro-business, neoliberal centre ground.' Labour hated the idea that the SNP were flying a false flag, and were determined prove that they were truly Tartan Tories.

Actually, the worst thing about the Full Fiscal Autonomy 'bombshell' as Labour depicted it – following the Tories' tax bombshell of the 1990s – was that the campaign was almost entirely negative. Project Fear may have been enough to win the referendum, but a General Election is a different matter. The negativity occluded Labour's positive pledges: the funding for eighteen year olds, increased minimum wage, anti-poverty fund etc. All it did was remind Scottish voters of Jim Murphy's collaboration with the Conservatives in Better Together. It was a disastrous campaign. If the Tories did the SNP's job for them, then Labour provided much of the spadework.

FULL FISCAL CONFUSION

It has to be said that the SNP was intellectually weak on the finances of fiscal autonomy. Nicola Sturgeon was perhaps justified in arguing that it wasn't an election issue, because Full Fiscal Autonomy was not on the cards, and that the immediate issue was 'Tory austerity cuts'. But they never fully rebutted the charge that there would indeed be a financial shortfall if all tax raising were to be devolved to Holyrood. The Scottish press made a great deal of this and placed the Institute for

Fiscal Studies' findings regularly on the front pages.[21]

Comment pieces and editorials hammered home the message that the economics of fiscal autonomy were no more sound than the economics of independence. Indeed, the Scottish and UK press started using much the same rhetorical themes – black holes, fiscal deficits, collapsing oil revenues – as during the independence referendum campaign. The only headline they didn't repeat was the 'New Blow for Salmond/ Sturgeon' since that had become a running joke on Twitter.

However, FFA was the dog that didn't bark in the general election. This was probably because the voters, and politicians, became confused by an increasingly complex set of overlapping statistical arguments. The Institute of Fiscal Studies also claimed in widely publicised reports that there were financial 'black holes' in both the Tory and Labour spending plans.[22] As these further reports emerged, what might be called a law of diminishing black holes set in. The tax expert Richard Murphy accused the IFS of being biased in favour of austerity economics.[23] The political parties then turned on the Institute and claimed that it had got its figures wrong.[24] In 2015, the distinguished think tank became too close to the political action for comfort, and risked becoming renamed the Institute for Fiscal Confusion.

I believe that Scots did get the message that fiscal autonomy, like independence, would be no walk in the park. They could understand the Institute of Fiscal Studies' similar basic argument about independence being a project with many financial imponderables. However, they also concluded that fiscal autonomy was not going to happen overnight as a result of this general election because Westminster was opposed to it. Many also preferred to believe the assurances of Nicola Sturgeon that Scotland was quite capable of 'managing its own affairs' in the long term like other countries, and that the Institute of Fiscal Studies were just a set of unionist gloomsters. Sturgeon's personal authority was a huge factor here. Labour were not just dealing with a resurgent nationalism, they were dealing with one of the most formidable personalities in contemporary politics.

The unionist parties had hoped to undermine the SNP in the election campaign by equating the party with Alex Salmond, a marmite politician who is loathed in England and regarded with some suspicion by many in Scotland. Early Tory election billboards depicted a smirking Salmond with Ed Miliband poking out of his top pocket. But they soon found themselves dealing not with Salmond, but with a politician who carries none of his baggage and has a rare ability to connect across gender and class boundaries. Sharp, intelligent, confident, down to earth: Nicola Sturgeon's image chimed with how modern Scots like to regard themselves.

Unionist newspapers had to swallow their loathing of the SNP and put her on the front pages day after day because she was simply so popular with their readers. Here was powerful Nicola in her smart red dress at her manifesto launch; smiling Nicola taking selfies with nice old ladies; talking to crowds of women in George Square; exercising in a gymnasium; and grinning with small children in a Wendy House. Nicola, as everyone calls her in Scotland, has the gift of being able to convey a political message simply by being there. This means she doesn't always need to engage in the rough and tumble of conventional political argument.

So, when Jim Murphy scored some real hits in the TV debates, for example over her apparent equivocation over calling another referendum (she was booed over this at the Scottish Leaders Debate on April 7th after her only serious mistake), it did little or no damage.[25] This was immensely frustrating for Murphy. Labour critics took to calling her 'Saint Nicola' on the grounds that she could apparently do no wrong and because the Scottish voters seemed to worship her. Nicola Sturgeon's net approval rating at close of play was plus 48, against minus 18 for Jim Murphy, and minus 46 for

Ed Miliband. This is extraordinary for a politician who is not only a serving First Minister, but has been on the ministerial front line for a full eight years. In the *Herald* on 12th April, after yet another of her many TV debates, I wrote: 'The voters of Scotland seem to have fallen in love with Nicola Sturgeon; she is adored. And while love affairs with politicians rarely last, this one only has to endure four short weeks.'

Reflecting on this assessment, I think now there was more to this than simply a political personality at the top of her game. Ms Sturgeon's appeal has something in common with that of leaders of the European populist left movements like Pablo Iglesias of Podemos in Spain and Alexis Tsipras of Syriza in Greece. She is a modern social democrat seeking a broad national opposition to austerity economics. The explosive growth of the SNP, led by the urban working class turning away from the traditional parties of the Left, echoes the way Syriza displaced the Greek Socialist Party PSOE. Like the European populists, the SNP kept its message simple: 'Scotland's voice stronger in Westminster', and Sturgeon is not afraid to use her own image to convey a political message. She brought star quality to politics in a way we haven't seen in Scotland for many years. The Scottish voters, in their current almost festive mood of political optimism, couldn't get enough of her.

We cannot draw too many comparisons with European nationalisms because of the particular constitutional situation in the UK. But the terms of Nicola Sturgeon's 'mission statement' in this election will be familiar to many throughout Europe:

My role is to build a Scotland that all those who live and work here can be proud of, a nation both social democratic and socially just, a Scotland confident in itself, proud of its successes and honest about its weaknesses, a Scotland of good government and civic empowerment.

These sentiments may be dismissed as the clichés of modern populist politics, but they captured the imagination of Scottish voters. The inability of the unionist parties to match these aspirations has plunged the UK into its worst ever crisis.

British politics used to be defined by class; it is now increasingly defined by nation. In place of the old binary UK elections offering a choice of Labour versus Conservative with a side order of Liberal, Britain is now a multinational/ multiparty democracy. The Scottish National Party is now the leading edge of Scottish politics; the Conservative Party is the lead in England. But this is not a clash of cultural or ethnic nationalisms. Nor is it merely about 'identity' – Scots have been quite secure about their identity within the United Kingdom. The divergence between north and south is based on profound differences of political culture.

The SNP is a party of the European Left, standing for increased social protections, an end to nuclear weapons, proportional representation, a socially responsible European Union, higher taxes on the wealthy, and liberal immigration policies. Under David Cameron, the most right-wing UK Conservative government since the 1980s pursues an agenda of spending cuts, a freeze on personal taxation, renewal of Trident, and retreat from Europe. The tensions between Holyrood and Westminster can only grow.

SCOTLAND DECIDES

In the final stages of the campaign, Labour was reduced to appealing to the older Conservative and middle class voters who had voted No in the referendum. This 'core vote' strategy was anything but, since Labour's working class core vote in the cities of Scotland had defected en masse to the SNP. Labour's lapse into the negative rhetoric of Better Together only accelerated this meltdown of Labour's true core.[26] The unionist newspapers believed that only tactical voting could stop the SNP now.[27] But the warnings about fiscal autonomy weren't working any more. Labour's campaign simply failed to connect with what had been happening in Scotland since the referendum, which it is now clear was a crucible in which attitudes to the Union were transformed and a new Scottish polity emerged.

The civic engagement that fuelled the referendum campaign and motivated 97% of Scots to register to vote was still there. Scottish voters had been told after the No vote that they had to get back in their box, pack away the festival of democracy, and return to the normality of boring responsible politics. But the people refused to get back in their box, or to seek consolation in negativity and cynicism. They looked around themselves, found that the world hadn't come to an end, and went right on keeping on. People are still coming out in their thousands to talk politics in pubs, town halls, theatres, and book festivals. I've spoken to many of them myself, and it is difficult not to be infected with their enthusiasm. Armed with the Internet, seized by a sense of communal purpose, the people of Scotland refuse to believe that a better society is impossible.

Scots were enjoying themselves too. They've taken to politics in the way people used to follow football. Indeed, there is something of the Tartan Army in the legions of raucously partisan SNP followers on the Internet, only the discourse is rather less male dominated. This, of course, horrifies the political establishment and its scribes, who regarded nationalism as a dangerous lapse into emotion and unreason. 'The Scots have gone mad,' said columnists like Chris Deerin and Iain Martin.[28] The establishment always rings the alarm when the people start to take history into their own hands. But this civic madness is surely no more irrational than the civic activism of the past – of the Chartists, the Suffragettes, the

Civil Rights Movement.

Labour insisted that it was Scottish voters' duty to remain in the Union for the sake of those less fortunate than themselves. This was a familiar refrain of metropolitan left-wing commentary on the rise of the SNP. 'Shared values are more important than borders,' said the *Guardian*'s columnist Polly Toynbee, 'social democrats are better together, confronting a common enemy.'[29]

But Scottish voters were tired of being told that it is somehow indecent to support a nationalist party, even though it seemed more socialist than anything else on offer. They were fed up being scolded by Labour politicians like Gordon Brown for abandoning the poor and dispossessed of northern England, as if Scottish voters were in some way responsible for Westminster policies since Thatcherism. Above all, they were tired of being told that they should unthinkingly support a Labour Party, which had for many years been a hollow and even corrupt shell in Scotland, and in England was a playground for special interests and commercial lobby groups.

Nicola Sturgeon speaks with confidence about her party's commitment to progressive change because she believes it, but mainly because she is leading hundreds of thousands of Scottish voters who refuse to give up on the possibility of change. Those voters will not willingly lapse back into apathy and retail politics, which is handed to them by the press and the Westminster establishment. Nicola has become the figurehead and the personification of a civic renewal movement that has been sweeping Scotland during the crucial years of 2014/15. As the new SNP MP Tommy Sheppard put it, the tsunami was 'not a political swing in the normal sense but a structural shift in political alignments across Scotland'.

Historians will marvel, not only at the unprecedented scale of the SNP's tidal 30% swing, but that it was so uniform. There has never been an electoral shift quite like this before in the British Isles, not even in Ireland which was riven with a sectarian religious divide. The SNP swept the board almost everywhere in Scotland: from snooty middle class Edinburgh to streetwise Glasgow; from the wealthy landed estates of Perthshire to the impoverished housing estates of the inner cities; from the echoing Highlands in the far north to Walter Scott's rolling Scottish Borders; from oil-rich Aberdeen in the East to the lonely islands off Scotland's West coast. The 2015 General Election seemed to unify Scotland by wiping away political, religious, class, and geographical divisions, in one extraordinary electoral moment. It was, by any definition, a revolutionary event, even though no one was harmed in the course of it.

Well, except perhaps for the Labour leader Jim Murphy. It was his misfortune to have been the wrong politician in the wrong place at the wrong time, as Labour's fifty-year hegemony came crashing to an end. As I wrote in the *Herald* on the weekend before the ground shifted: 'Nelson Mandela himself could not have turned around Labour's fortunes in these few short months. We are seeing a political sea change, a generational transformation and a national awakening all at the same time. In this election, unlike any before, it's all about Scotland.'

Chapter Two:

Mr Sheppard Goes to Westminster

The early April wind was raw on Restalrig Road in Edinburgh's East side as Tommy Sheppard hauled his bulky frame out of his black Volvo cabriolet for the first round of canvassing of the weekend. The fifty-six year old is the SNP candidate for Edinburgh East, one of the safest Labour seats in the country, where the sitting MP Sheila Gilmore has a majority of over 11,000. The previous night Mr Sheppard had presided over a rather glamorous fundraiser organised by his constituency party and featuring some well-known Scottish stand-up comedians. This was back to reality with a bump.

Edinburgh East is a sprawling constituency that includes Scotland's top tourist attraction, Edinburgh Castle, as well as Holyrood Palace and the Scottish Parliament. But it also encompasses the most socially deprived area of Scotland's capital city, Craigmillar, which used to be Edinburgh's largest housing estate before they started demolishing large parts of it. In the 1980s, this was the epicentre of Edinburgh's hard drug scene, immortalised by Irvine Welsh in *Trainspotting*. Craigmillar still has serious drug and alcohol problems and is currently number four in Scotland's 'Index of Multiple Deprivation'. Edinburgh East, under various boundaries, has in living memory been forever Labour.

Sheppard is the co-founder and director of The Stand comedy clubs in Scotland and Newcastle. He set up his first club in Edinburgh in 1998 with redundancy money from the Labour Party, of which he had been Assistant Secretary to Jack McConnell, who went on to be First Minister of Scotland. When he lived in London prior to that he had been deputy leader of Labour controlled Hackney council. That was then. Now Sheppard was the SNP candidate for Edinburgh East, one of the many to invade the SNP after the referendum. He says he didn't leave the Labour Party – it left him.

He had organised the star-studded 'Night for Scotland' concert in Edinburgh's Usher Hall four days before the referendum vote, but why did he join the SNP five days after independence was defeated? I asked him as we waited for the team of SNP canvassers to arrive: 'Well, it seemed the right moment. I'd been thinking [about it] while working in the Yes Scotland campaign. It's the only way forward. I could see Labour were finished.'

Isn't the culture of the SNP as a party different from the Labour left? 'Not really. There's a lot of people like me. The membership in Edinburgh East aren't that different from the people I used to see in Labour. I found my first SNP branch meetings only too similar to the Labour branch meetings I attended twenty years ago.'

Like many of the new generation of SNP candidates, Sheppard appears to regard the SNP as the direct descendant of Labour and, of course, it never occurs to him that his lack of Scottish roots makes any difference – he was born in Coleraine in Northern Ireland. But would he have thought that of the SNP back when he was a Hackney councillor? What about the older romantic nationalists who revere Wallace and Bruce and don't much like the English – aren't there still a few of them around? 'Well, if there are they keep their heads well down,' he says. 'The new members aren't like that. We're not a bunch of people coming down on the Megabus to London in kilts and waving claymores.'

Like most Scottish SNP constituency parties, Edinburgh East's membership more than quadrupled in the months after the referendum and now stands at around 1800 members. Success brought problems for the SNP leadership. Suddenly, they didn't know who the vast majority of their new party members were, what they thought, what they expected. Tommy Sheppard got to know by telephoning 1200 of them personally in the Edinburgh East Constituency Association to ask for their support in the candidate selection process earlier this year. He won overwhelmingly.

In November 2014, the SNP scrapped its long-standing rule that new members had to wait at least a year before they could be considered general election candidates. It was an astute move. It allowed the SNP to place capable non-nationalists in hitherto 'unwinnable' seats like Edinburgh East. Opening the doors also put some substance to the party's claim to be an open-minded, non-doctrinaire party, the inheritor of broad-based, non-sectarian social democracy in Scotland. Anyway, in this election no seat in Scotland was safe any more, and who better to stand against the moribund Labour Party than a former senior Labour official? Not everyone in the Edinburgh East SNP, or in the party generally, was entirely happy with this rule change, however, since it meant that many stalwart party workers found themselves upstaged by newcomers. One disgruntled rival started a poisonous social media campaign against Sheppard, until he stamped it out.

I meet another of Sheppard's former rivals, the runner-up in the Edinburgh East selection contest, Lloyd Quinan, at the Niddrie Mains offices next to the Craigmillar branch of Lidl. The former TV weatherman had been an SNP activist since 1974 and is a former member of the Scottish Parliament, though he defected for a while to the Scottish Socialist Party. But if he's sore at losing, he doesn't show it. Quinan is raving about the canvas returns in Bingham, one of the most socially deprived areas of the constituency, which the SNP has invaded like a conquering army. They're getting returns of over 70% here. I rarely believe what canvassers say about their returns, but he shows me the lists identifying all the switchers from Labour. 'It was the referendum campaign that did it,' Quinan says, having worked closely with the Yes Campaign before

September 2014. 'That's when people who hadn't talked about politics for years started discussing it, and they just didn't stop.' SNP canvassers here recount similar anecdotes about being on doorsteps with family members who had never actually spoken to each other before about politics, discovering that they no longer knew why they voted Labour – if they voted at all.

DOORSTEPPING THE SWITHERERS

The SNP stall back in blowy Restalrig Road looked singularly unimpressive. A handful of people minding a trestle table with piles of leaflets held down with stones, and a few bobbing yellow balloons. This didn't feel like a revolution. Two hundred yards up the road Sheppard's Labour rival was posing in front of large 'Sheila Gilmore' posters, surrounded apparently by throngs of eager supporters. She seemed to be attracting a lot more interest than the SNP – or perhaps they were flying supporters brought in for the photo-shoot. They melted away afterwards and I didn't see any Labour canvassers for the rest of the day.

There were seven of these little SNP outposts across the sprawling Edinburgh East constituency that Saturday morning. On paper it looked like a hopeless cause. Sheppard's SNP predecessor, the prominent Scottish journalist George Kerevan, considered it an achievement to reach 20% of the vote here in 2010, which meant Sheppard needed a swing of something approaching 20% – a ridiculous objective in a general election. Restalrig Road is deep in Labour territory and there is a degree of trepidation as the canvassers load their clip-boards with lists delivered for them by the Activate computerised canvassing system used by the SNP.

Canvassing is a science. Every known resident on the electoral register is given a score of 1 to 8 based on how likely they are to vote, or not vote, SNP. The task on this round is to identify those who might be swithering from their support for Labour. They would then be followed up by literature drops and further doorstepping. The known SNP and Yes supporters are ignored, though they get 'motivational material' later. No point wasting time on those already persuaded. It seems a little unfair somehow. But Sheppard tells me firmly: 'the SNP is the only party that deliberately goes after the people who do not already support it.'

Restalrig Road is one of those diverse Edinburgh streets that seems to be a demographic résumé of Scotland. Within a couple of hundred yards you go from rather shabby 30s council blocks, through private terraces with B&Q doors and white vans decked with tradesmen's logos. Next are some of those echoing Edwardian tenements often occupied by young professionals and older, working class couples. Finally, you arrive at a stretch of imposing sandstone villas with stone lions sitting in front of them.

At first there seems to be no one at home. But as the hours pass, the doors begin to open as we dodge the spring hailstorms. I expect a degree of resentment from residents at being bothered by canvassers on their weekends, but I'm wrong. Most people who answer their doors seem quite eager to talk, even some of the Labour voters (though Tommy suspects they are just trying to waste canvasser time). In this street people are clearly in switching mood, and a number switch from Labour to SNP on the doorstep.

Most people think tramping around a wet constituency getting the occasional door slammed in your face must be torture, but it makes politics literally come alive. You realise that voters aren't just statistical categories, numbers juggled by Professor John Curtice. They may not all have university degrees and may not be up to speed on the minutiae of full fiscal autonomy but most voters take their democratic responsibility very seriously. And they are much more intelligent than most academics, and certainly most journalists, give them credit for; especially those commentators who were saying during the 2015 election that Scottish voters have been 'swayed by short-term emotion rather than rational thinking'.[30] It would have been interesting to take a walk down Restalrig Road with David Blunkett, the former Labour cabinet minister who told the BBC with extraordinary arrogance: 'I think their [Scots'] minds have switched off to even rational argument.'[31] The voters here would have given Mr Blunkett something to think about.

The political sophistication of Scottish voters came as no surprise to me, however. I came face to face with it during the referendum campaign when I found myself inadvertently talking about arcane aspects of monetary policy with total strangers in supermarket queues and on buses. I travelled the length and breadth of Scotland in 2014 and found that people were talking about politics in the way they usually talk about football or celebrity culture. They still are. I travelled around Scotland again during the 2015 General Election promoting my book *Disunited Kingdom* (Cargo, 2014) and found the same enthusiasm for change – only more resolute, it seemed. Scottish voters have been through an extraordinary learning curve in the past three years. They are fully aware of the arguments, determined to seek that 'better nation', and have been thinking very seriously about how to achieve it.

I would have liked to spend more time talking but at this stage in a campaign canvassers don't really want to engage in lengthy discussion. They want to identify quickly who might be worth following up and which houses can be safely ignored in the future. 'And what party do you normally identify with?' is Tommy Sheppard's standard opening gambit. People don't like being asked cold how they voted in a general election – it sounds intrusive – but they don't mind talking in hypotheticals. A number say they've never been canvassed before. The main thing that seems to concern Edinburgh East voters is the risk of another referendum. 'That's all the SNP cares about' is a common observation from sceptics. I don't hear anyone talk about full fiscal autonomy despite the fact that the papers that day had been full of reports about the Institute of Fiscal Studies' warning that Scotland faced a £7.6bn shortfall if it adopted the SNP's policy of devolving all taxation to Scotland. Many say that they have thought about voting SNP, but aren't sure about going through 'all that again', meaning the referendum. Sheppard advises them that 'this election isn't about another referendum' – which is true, but it doesn't always convince.

The personality of Nicola Sturgeon is clearly a big advantage. Even Labour supporters seem incapable of disliking her. I notice that people seem to smile as soon as her name is mentioned, as if she is a personal friend. On the other hand, the frustration about Labour and 'Westminster politicians' is almost palpable. It is a resentment bordering on anger in some cases, and for not entirely explicable reasons since in policy terms there isn't all that much difference between the SNP and Labour manifestos. But the remoteness of establishment politics, its apparent corruption, and the narrow obsessions of the UK media, seem to have a lot to do with the growing disenchantment. Whatever else it did, the 'Vow' delivered by the unionist parties in the dying days of the independence referendum did not reassure voters that they had 'got' Scotland.

There are, of course, still many solid Labour voters in East Edinburgh, though they tend to be older and wealthier. It is one of the paradoxes of Scottish politics that the Labour Party has tended to be the party of the middle classes in many urban areas that would be Conservative in England. Tommy doesn't get a great reception on the doorsteps of the sandstone villas on the whole. They aren't all hostile, but most say that he is wasting his time. Still, by then he's pretty satisfied with the morning's work.

MONEY TALKS

A couple of days later, and another fundraiser: this time at a local restaurant where the star speaker was to be one Alex Salmond. He is over an hour late. Sheppard, and the chair of the session, Jeane Freeman of Women for Independence, have to deliver inordinately lengthy warm-up speeches as the 150 audience eat rather dry sandwiches. Sheppard is a strong platform speaker, as he demonstrated at the SNP's pre-election conference when he received a rousing welcome from his new party. But this isn't one of his better efforts. He hasn't fully mastered the knack of delivering claptrap – the stock phrases and rhetorical climaxes that force audiences to applaud on cue. But he says he doesn't like talking down to audiences, and, though it sounds like a seminar on civic engagement, they seem to get it.

Alex Salmond eventually arrives and proceeds to talk almost entirely about his own book, *The Dream Shall Never Die*, which he also happens to be promoting. He boasts that it has been topping the *Sunday Times* bestseller list for three weeks. Salmond delivers anecdotes about his campaign in Gordon where he is hoping to return as MP to Westminster. Seeing the odd journalist, he is careful to name-check Nicola Sturgeon and avoid too many jokes. The former first minister got into trouble at one recent private event when he said that he would be 'writing Labour's next Budget'.[32] He speaks at length about the honorary degree from Glasgow University he is about to receive that evening, before eventually getting round to mentioning the merits of the Edinburgh East candidate. The guests, who had paid £15 for the privilege, don't seem disappointed.

Fundraising is a top priority for SNP candidates. The SNP has no structural links with trade unions or big business so, unlike Labour, it doesn't receive millions from Unison,

GMB, and Unite. The Conservatives can rely on hedge fund billionaires like Sir Michael Hintze.[33] The SNP has had a couple of individual donors like the Stagecoach magnate Brian Souter, and the lottery winners, Colin and Chris Weir, who largely financed the Yes Scotland campaign. But during the first two weeks of the 'short campaign' in 2015, the SNP received no gifts of more than £7,500 according to the Electoral Commission.[34] Most of its cash comes from its 105,000 members, which is not a bad business model for a party whose membership has more than quadrupled in the past year.

The SNP claim that this shows how a genuine grass-roots democracy can and should be financed: by legions of ordinary members and supporters. People are money. 150 folk turning up to hear Alex Salmond can raise up to £3000 one way or another. Throughout his campaign, Sheppard organised weekly events at the Radical Road pub in Willowbrae Road. Even Nicola Sturgeon's televised debates were turned into fundraising events. Using his membership as a base, Sheppard raised £18,000, about half from members' subs, and half from fundraising events. Most was spent on printing his campaign newspaper, leaflets, and election address. Then there were three campaign offices, street stalls, and merchandising like T-shirts and badges. He received no additional funds from the SNP centrally, or from any trade union.

At a hustings event at Portobello Town Hall the next night, Tommy Sheppard is in his element. The hall is packed and there are constituents looking down from the gallery above. This election and the referendum before it has seen the revival of town hall politics in a way unseen in Scotland for at least thirty years. It is an unusually rowdy crowd and the chair of the local community council has a tough job keeping order. People have rediscovered what previous generations of voters always knew: that politics is a participation sport and can be fun.

The seven candidates in Edinburgh East are lined up on the stage like targets in a shooting gallery. Sheppard sits expressionless at the left of the panel next to the Ukip candidate who doesn't seem to be entirely sure where he is. Sheppard's main rival, Labour's Sheila Gilmore, sits dead centre. She is the only one who stands when she is called to give her two-minute pitch. It is a competent but rather pedestrian account of her work for the constituency, as if she was up for an annual appraisal – which perhaps she is. There is polite applause, and some heckling about Labour endorsing austerity. Peter McColl, the Green Party candidate, has a significant following in the room and delivers a clever and amusing speech which majors on social justice themes and the party proposal for a £10 minimum wage rather than the environment. But Sheppard gets the biggest cheers of the night. He is fluent and confident, using his former position in the Labour party as his USP, claiming that the SNP is the best hope for social democracy, not just for Scotland but for the UK.

The crowd is more middle class and bohemian in Portobello and there are questions about issues like fracking that you don't often hear on the doorsteps of Restalrig. When candidates are asked to give an example of where and when they might defy their party whip, Sheppard replies: 'fracking is precisely the kind of decision adversely affecting the constituency that I might vote against. I hope they don't throw me out,' he adds, laughing. The previous month there had been some controversy over a motion passed at the SNP conference banning candidates from speaking in public against party policy if they are elected to parliament. Labour and press commentators suggested that this was a sign of authoritarian centralism in the SNP.

I ask Sheppard about this later and he laughs again. 'Every party tells MPs they have to vote with the party whip, Labour certainly did. Doesn't mean they always do.' But hasn't the SNP made it clear that you can't remain if you don't tow the line? I ask. 'No one sets out to defy their party line but sometimes you might have to,' he replies. 'But you need to be prepared to face the consequences.'

All the prospective SNP candidates were of course vetted by the party centrally to ensure that they were capable, understood party policy, and had no skeletons in their cupboard. They only made one serious mistake and that was in the neighbouring constituency of Edinburgh South. The candidate, Neil Hay, was revealed to have been a so-called 'cybernat' with the moniker Paco McSheepie, who had made some disrespectful comments about older No voters. That cost him the support of the First Minister, Nicola Sturgeon, who did not sack Hay but conspicuously failed to defend him. Had it not been for that error of judgment by the SNP's candidate selection, Labour might not have returned its only MP, Ian Murray, on May 7th.

A week later and we're canvassing a very different area of East Edinburgh called The Jewel, in a street with the intriguing name, Parrotshot. The Jewel was a rich coal seam that used to run under what is now called Niddrie, and Parrotshot was a particularly flammable bituminous coal. This used to be mining country. It's now one of those new build owner-occupier estates that UK Labour leadership candidates call 'aspirational working class'. The houses are small but detached, as if someone had sliced up a terrace and edged the units apart. The cul de sacs are littered with children's toys and cars. This is the kind of area that would probably be Conservative or Ukip in the South East of England, and solidly Labour further north. But here support for the SNP is spreading door to door like a fashion.

Around 50% of the doors we visit are now SNP. If you take out the people who say they aren't going to vote at all, that means a 70% canvas return – and this of course excludes the known SNP and Yes voters who don't get canvassed at this stage. The ones who are persuaded to back Sheppard sound as if they can't quite remember why they never voted SNP before. At one point a voter jogs down the road to chat with Sheppard because he hadn't been in when we knocked. It's the first time I've ever seen a politician being chased down the street by a voter in a good way. Sheppard offers him a couple of 'VOTE SHEPPARD' posters to put in his windows, which he accepts as if they're prizes. The value of face-to-face meetings with constituents could hardly have been better illustrated than on these windy weekend mornings.

In The Jewel there are a number of Labour voters who seem to have lost faith but can't quite make the switch to the SNP and need persuaded. Some say they don't feel at ease being classed as nationalists. Tommy gently cajoles them, insisting that this election is about giving Scotland a stronger voice in Westminster. 'This election is not about independence,' is again his doorstep mantra. He gives some of them his personal phone number in case they want to discuss it further.

Are you really a nationalist? I ask him later. He tosses his head as if surprised. 'No, I'm not a nationalist. I'm an internationalist.' But isn't this a nationalist party? 'I think there's lots of people in the SNP who aren't really nationalists. Or rather are civic nationalists who see themselves first of all as social democrats. For me, independence is a means to the same ends in which I've always believed.'

But would you go to the annual Bannockburn celebrations? 'Not willingly... I suppose if I was asked to speak, but I wouldn't think of going on my own initiative.'

Are you interested in Scottish history, in the wars of independence? He shrugs. I get the impression that Wallace and Robert the Bruce would not be Tommy Sheppard's special subject on Mastermind.

SNP candidates find this line of questioning a little offensive, as if you are trying to pigeonhole them as anti-English Braveheart fanatics. You might as well suggest they are racist. Some of Tommy's former Labour colleagues, like the former leader of Scottish Labour Action Ian Smart, call some SNP members 'fascist scum'.[35] There is understandable sensitivity about the historical reputation of nationalism in Europe after the disasters of the twentieth century, and given the right-wing character of many nationalist parties in Europe today. But the SNP is still a nationalist movement, a civic nationalist movement certainly, but nationalist nevertheless. I come from a very similar background to Tommy Sheppard and, like most on the Left, used to be instinctively hostile to the very word 'nationalism'. My late mother was National Secretary of the SNP in the 1970s and I used to taunt her with the old leftist line; 'SNP. BNP. There's only one letter different.' I regret that now. She had joined the party in the 1960s after Labour reneged on its promise to abolish nuclear weapons. She remained, essentially because it was the only left-wing party she had been involved with in which women were expected to do more than make the tea. It was the party of Winnie Ewing and Margo Macdonald. Our house in Edinburgh was filled with radical nationalist voices like the late Stephen Maxwell, author of *The Case for Left Wing Nationalism*.

What had Wallace and Bruce to do with this modern civic nationalist movement? Well, quite a lot actually, as I realised when I went back to the National Question in Scotland while researching my 2013 book *Road to Referendum*. Of course, the Scottish Wars of Independence have little direct relevance to the political circumstances of today, except in this respect: that their actions seven hundred years ago did ensure that Scotland remained a nation and was not merged into the Anglo-French Plantagenet empire. The Scottish rebellion was one of the earliest nationalist movements in an era – the late Middle Ages – of continental dynasties. It was not a democratic movement because the concept of democracy was alien to feudal society. But the Declaration of Arbroath in 1320 remains a defiant statement against tyranny and divine right. It said, essentially, that if King Robert I didn't shape up, the 'community of the realm' had every right to replace him with someone who did.

That assertion of national independence led to another 400 years of conflict with England. But it meant that the union of 1707 was not an annexation but a partnership – at least in theory – in which Scotland traded formal political independence for security and economic advantage. But the country was not extinguished. It retained its distinct institutional existence in the form of the Kirk, the education system, and the law. Scotland remained a nation and did not become a colony of England. I fully understand the reluctance to celebrate bloody conflict with England. 'Scots wha hae wi' Wallace bled' and so forth. But this is not a history to be ashamed of, any more than the Magna Carta, the English Reformation or the Glorious Revolution.

And it is an important dimension of the SNP's current success in Scotland. There is a presence of the past here. It is surely partly because of that history that voters in Parrotshot and Restalrig had been so receptive to the appeal of the SNP during and after the referendum. They weren't all utilitarian nationalists, just wanting a better Labour Party. Their sense of right and justice is based on a communal sense of belonging to a nation. A nation with strong communitarian and social democratic values, certainly, but a nation nevertheless. Nationalism and democracy are not mutually exclusive – historically they have generally gone hand in hand, as the civic revolutionary Tom Paine made clear in pamphlets like *Common Sense* advocating the American Revolution 200 years ago.

At any rate, the voters in East Edinburgh seem to have 'got' nationalism by a form of communitarian osmosis. They certainly didn't get it from the Scottish press which has been overwhelmingly unionist and in whose pages – curiously for a national media – discussion of Scottish history is almost entirely absent. Scotland's conversion to Scottish nationalism has been a social as much as a political phenomenon. And it seems clear that for many of the 1.4 million Scots who voted SNP it has ceased being a decision based purely on comparison of manifestos. Support for independence is no longer something that needs to be debated or questioned or interrogated; it has become self-evident. It's what you do.

Labour friends will throw up hands in horror at this thought. Mindless nationalism – what next? But I don't necessarily see anything unique or disturbing about this. During the miners' strike in 1984, when people still knew The Jewel wasn't a precious stone, many of these same communities were just as certain about the importance of the trade union, cause and opposing Thatcherism. It was called working class solidarity. What the SNP seems to have achieved in East Edinburgh, as in so many working class communities in Scotland, is to have fused class solidarity with a latent sense of national identity so that many voters can still feel they're in touch with their Labour roots even though they are voting SNP. This isn't about identity as such – Scots have rarely had a problem with their identity. Rather, they have, for a variety of reasons, started to feel a degree of self-confidence about it.

TOMMY TRIUMPHANT

Labour activists weren't feeling very self-confident on election night at the Edinburgh count. The declaration wasn't until 5am but Sheppard knew soon after the ballot boxes had been opened that he had won – and by a large margin. He had overturned the safest Labour seat in Edinburgh with a majority of 9,106 on an astonishing 29% swing. Those SNP canvassers I had suspected of indulging in wishful thinking were bang on the money. The time spent tramping Parrotshot and Restalrig had not been wasted. Sheppard received 49.2% of the votes. Labour had held Edinburgh East under its previous boundaries since 1924, and only once had less than 40% of the vote here.

Election results do not come more dramatic than this.

In a city where 65% of voters had voted No in the independence referendum, this was clearly a result with national resonance, and Sheppard's acceptance speech had a suitably historic ring to it. 'Something remarkable has happened in Scotland tonight,' he said to ecstatic SNP supporters. 'Politics in Scotland has changed completely and forever. Things will never ever be the same again.' Labour supporters shook their heads indignantly as he claimed that 'for the first time in our history we send a majority of political representatives to the Union parliament whose first and only mandate will come from the communities who elected them and whose ambition will not be compromised by being part of the Westminster Establishment.'

Sheppard said his vote was a mandate to oppose austerity, nuclear weapons, and food banks, and he repeated his doorstep riff about this election not being about independence. But he warned the political establishment that the constitution was not to be taken for granted. 'If we are to remain in the United Kingdom, Scotland will no longer be seen and not heard…this has been an expression of national self-confidence. We take that mandate, but we take it with humility and we understand the preciousness of the trust the Scottish people have placed in us.'

Non-nationalists at the Edinburgh count thought he had gone over the top, got above himself. Sheila Gilmore made dry reference in her speech about how being an MP was about hard work, not 'big speeches'. It wasn't hard to understand the bewilderment of the former Labour MP for Edinburgh East. Here was someone from her own Labour background stealing her constituency under a false flag, as she would see it. Tommy Sheppard was one of the young radicals who formed Scottish Labour Action in the 90s along with Jack McConnell and Wendy Alexander. 'I'm the only one left, and here I am' he told me.

Sheila Gilmore was by no means the worst Labour MP to lose their seat in the massacre of the 7th of May. She was an uncharismatic MP who, nevertheless, had served her constituents diligently since 2010 as they faced unemployment and financial hardship. Now she was the one looking for a job. Though perhaps she should have understood the dynamics of civic nationalism rather better. Gilmore, a solicitor, had apparently been a member of the breakaway Scottish Labour Party set up by Jim Sillars in the 1970s.

WHO ARE THE '56'?

In many ways Sheppard typifies the new SNP parliamentary group by being so atypical. He is ex-Labour, a businessman, a socialist, and an internationalist. He told me that one of his priorities as a Westminster MP would be campaigning for human and political rights for the people of Palestine. The 56 Scottish National Party MPs who made their way in triumph to Westminster on May 11th 2015, infuriating the Palace authorities by taking selfies in the chamber, are indeed a diverse bunch.

Many are very new to politics like Philippa Whitford, the prominent breast cancer surgeon and relentless opponent of market-based reforms in the NHS. 'This is going to be the most non-political group of politicians Westminster has seen' she told the *Guardian*: 'We are a bunch of mavericks.'[36] Attention has inevitably focused on some of the younger working class MPs, like Mhairi Black, the twenty-year-old politics student who defeated the former Labour foreign secretary, Douglas Alexander, in Paisley. Her selfie eating a chip butty on the Westminster Terrace was considered a breach of parliamentary etiquette and also led to criticism that the Nationalists were unserious juvenile rebels. But most of the SNP MPs are older – the average age is forty-five – and are middle class. About a third are senior SNP councillors, like Drew Hendry, the leader of Highland Council who beat the Treasury Secretary Danny Alexander in Inverness. There are a number of ex-TV journalists like John Nicholson in East Dunbartonshire (the Liberal Democrat minister Jo Swinson's old seat) who was a BBC presenter. Neil Gray in Airdrie and Hanna Bardell in Livingston are also former TV journalists, and Brendan O'Hara in Argyll is a TV documentary producer. Unlike Labour or the Conservative benches in Westminster, there is not a single Oxford or Cambridge graduate among the 56 Scottish National Party MPs. Only 5% were privately educated, according to the Sutton Trust.[37] They include: Edinburgh South-West's Joanna Cherry (St Margarets, Edinburgh), South Perthshire's Tasmina Ahmed-Sheikh (George Heriot's, Edinburgh) and Aberdeen North's Kirsty Blackman (Robert Gordon's, Aberdeen, on a scholarship). In the UK parliament as a whole, 33% of all MPs and 49% of Conservative MPs went to private schools.

Most of the new Scottish MPs claim to be of the left, but few have conventional left-wing backgrounds in trades unions or education. By no means all have emerged from the public or charitable sectors. According to an analysis in the *Financial Times,* six out of ten of the new intake have experience in the private sector and more than a quarter were in business.[38] Ian Blackford, who beat the former Liberal Democrat leader Charles Kennedy in Ross, Skye, and Lochaber, was an investment banker with Deutsche Bank. He had a reputation as a troublemaker in the SNP because he challenged Alex Salmond's expenses when he was National Treasurer in 2000. Michelle Thomson in Edinburgh West, another newcomer to politics, was a property consultant and senior figure in the pro-independence Business for Scotland.

Lawyer Tasmina Ahmed-Sheik, the MP for Ochil and a former Bollywood actress, is a former Conservative candidate as well as the only non-white SNP MP. George Kerevan of East Lothian was a former assistant editor of the *Scotsman* and, though once a Labour councillor, had a reputation as being conservative in his economic writings for the paper. Chris Law who won in Dundee West used to run a business organising motorbike tours in the Himalayas, and during the referendum drove a converted fire engine around Scotland proselytising for the cause of independence.

The Tory MP Owen Paterson's claim that the SNP are 'Marxists' is very wide of the mark.[39] However, what does perhaps define the new Scottish MPs is their commitment to gender politics. More than a third of the SNP's new intake are women and are strongly feminist. Natalie McGarry, who defeated the Shadow Scottish Secretary Margaret Curran in Glasgow East, co-founded the group Women for Independence – an organisation that fiercely insists on its separation both from the Yes Campaign and the SNP. She has few connections with the Labour movement and has a partner who is a Conservative councillor. Kirsten Oswald, who defeated the Scottish Labour leader Jim Murphy, is also a prominent activist in Women for Independence, and Joanna Cherry QC in Edinburgh South West is Scotland's first specialist sex crimes prosecutor.

It is indeed fascinating to speculate on where the ideological centre of this disparate grouping actually lies. We don't yet know their attitude on social issues like abortion, for example, though it is assumed because of the presence of feminists that the group supports it. Of course, they support party policy – they don't have any choice after that conference ruling – and that means they are signed up to utilitarian, social democratic nationalism. But few of them are clearly natural left-wingers in the hard Left sense. Nor are they really nationalists in the old-fashioned sense either. The Mac cartoon image of bearded, kilted Scotsmen ordering haggis in the Commons tearoom while playing the bagpipes couldn't be further from the reality.

I couldn't name a single member of the SNP group

who is a romantic nationalist of the kind who might, like the poet Hugh MacDiarmid, put 'anglophobia' as their hobby in *Who's Who*. There is little trace of ethnic nationalism either. I can't imagine MPs like George Kerevan turning up at a Bannockburn celebration wearing kilts and targes. Still less Jo Cherry or Natalie McGarry appearing with their faces painted at gatherings of 'the 45' or the Scottish Resistance. This generation of Scottish nationalists is very different from the old school, like Gordon Wilson, who claim that today's SNP lacks 'vision, passion and emotion' and should be attacking the 'southern cancer'.[40] They wouldn't have dreamed of stealing the Stone of Destiny or blowing up pillar boxes which had Elizabeth II on them.

Sensitivity to the charge from Labour that nationalism is all about race and division has made this generation of SNP intellectuals cautious about celebrating anything much to do with Scottish culture and history for fear they will be accused of ethnic exceptionalism. When I was in Westminster in the 1990s, Scottish Tory MPs like Bill Walker and Sir Nicholas Fairbairn flaunted their cultural identity and wore tartan at every opportunity. Even the former Scottish Secretary Michael Forsyth arranged for the Stone of Destiny to be returned to Scotland in 1996 in a wholly misguided attempt to appease Scotland's sense of nationhood. The irony of the modern SNP is that it is a party defined by national identity whose politics is almost wholly unconcerned with identity.

Yet there has been something of a popular cultural renaissance in Scotland over the last three decades. Tommy Sheppard has himself contributed to the revival of Scottish culture though his work for the Edinburgh Festival, and through promoting the careers of comedians like Frankie Boyle and Kevin Bridges, who both began performing in The Stand comedy clubs he founded. These stars have helped develop a new Scottish self-confidence simply by talking in a Scottish accent and making jokes about their own country.

Though they do have an unfortunate habit of reproducing crude social stereotypes in their comedy lines, as in Frankie Boyle's joke about the Braveheart actor Mel Gibson: 'Nobody thought he could play a Scot but now look at him. Alcoholic and a racist.' Or 'The English are worried about the euro being brought in because of loss of national identity and rising prices. In Scotland people are just worried in case they close Poundstretcher.'

They're funny, of course, and it is good that Scots laugh at themselves. Kevin Bridges tells a lot of jokes about Glasgow being advertised as the UK's friendliest city when it has such a reputation for violence. 'Come to Glasgow, you'll get the shit kicked out of you, but you'll get directions to the hospital.' But put the laughter to one side for a moment and you realise that this image is at variance with reality. 'No Mean City' has elected a string of feminists like Natalie McGarry and Alison Thewliss as its members of parliament, as well as the openly gay SNP MP Stewart McDonald in Glasgow South. The truth is that this is a much fairer representation of Glasgow, with its thriving gay community and its arts and music scene, than the grim machismo of Taggart, the fictional TV detective.

Indeed, the idea of Scotland as a dour and depressive country full of anger and resentment is one largely perpetuated by the UK media. It is what metropolitan publishers and newspaper editors want to see written about Scotland and there has never been any shortage of Scottish writers willing to provide the copy. But perhaps it is time for Scotland to put this all behind it now. If Scotland ever was this dark and violent land, it isn't any longer. Scotland has a drink problem but it's getting better. But, as the SNP MPs made their way to parliament, they were only too conscious that their cultural stereotypes had gone before them, as stories appeared about their welcome in the bars of the Palace of Westminster. The UK press fully expected that they would be boorish, difficult, disruptive, and the early breaches of parliamentary protocol seemed to confirm these expectations.

There was much tut-tutting in the press and among Labour politicians when the '56' made their presence felt in the Commons chamber by demanding that they were allowed to occupy the seats formerly held by the Liberal Democrats when they were the third party in opposition. The Father of the House, the Labour MP Sir Gerald Kaufman, called them 'goons'.[41] The veteran Labour MP Dennis Skinner said the seats row had made him forget to make one of his trademark sarcastic remarks during the State Opening of Parliament. But 'buttockburn' as it was called was soon resolved and Dennis kept his seat. The Scottish MPs swore their oaths of allegiance to the Queen without demur, even though a number are republicans.

The 56 Scottish SNP MPs are not only representatives. They are ambassadors of this new Scotland, and most of them are acutely aware of the responsibility they bear. The first SNP MP to deliver a maiden speech after the election, the Argyll MP Brendan O'Hara, struck what many Conservatives regarded as an unexpectedly conciliatory tone:

> For the first time ever, the four constituent parts of this United Kingdom delivered four very different verdicts on how this country should progress. This may seem like a circle that cannot be squared but our constituents expect us to find a way of working together constructively and that we must do.

Later, Tommy Sheppard's maiden speech to parliament delivered without notes on 28th May became something of a social media phenomenon. It had 56,000 views within the next four days, making it one of the most widely viewed maiden speeches in history. Written by him, and without any oversight from the party hierarchy, the speech again surprised commentators who believe the SNP is only in 'Westmonster' for the purposes of breaking up the UK at the earliest opportunity:

> We have not come to this chamber to argue the case for independence. That debate about the next chapter in Scotland's history will take place in a different chamber in a different parliament 400 miles north of this one. We have come here to give Scotland a strong voice in this parliament. We have come here to represent the people who elected us and we come here not to disrupt but to be constructively engaged and to be good parliamentarians.

Time will tell whether the SNP MPs find a way to make their presence truly felt in Westminster. They face a difficult task and, while they may believe that they hold many values in common with Labour, that does not mean they will necessarily be able to work with the official Opposition. On June 4th, Labour abstained on the first SNP's motion on the Queen's Speech condemning austerity. The main problem for the '56' may well be the frustration that radical voices often experience in Westminster. They will have to use intelligence and force of argument. But Scottish voters can be assured that, whatever else it does, this new force in Westminster politics will not remain silent.

Chapter Three:

Saint Nicola

The Edinburgh International Climbing Arena at Ratho is more like a James Bond film set than a political campaign venue. The largest of its kind in Europe, its 100 foot high walls were part of a disused quarry. Fifteen foot high artificial boulders litter the floor. It was here, on Monday 20th of April 2015, that Nicola Sturgeon made her most dramatic intervention on the UK political stage, launching the SNP manifesto 'Stronger for Scotland'. It could have gone horribly wrong.

This 'wee lassie wi' a tin helmet' as the Labour MP David Hamilton had described the First Minister, might have looked diminutive in these grandiose surroundings.[42] It was quite literally over the top – with the jagged edges of the climbing walls looming over her. What was she trying to say? That she is taking Scotland to the cliff edge? Was she planning a Matrix-style revolution? Predictably, the *Telegraph* columnist Iain Martin tweeted that it was a 'Nuremberg Rally'. But if she was overwhelmed by the surroundings, she didn't show it. The First Minister looked the largely unsympathetic UK press in the eye and delivered her text in her usual unflamboyant style, as if she spent most of her time making speeches in extra-terrestrial surroundings.

Sturgeon had already been addressing vast crowds in the months following the referendum defeat. She filled Scotland's largest entertainment venue, the Glasgow Hydro, on 22nd November 2014 with over 12,000 fans – not far short of the entire membership of the Scottish Labour Party. As in the Climbing Arena, her speech then was not an emotional, rousing flight of rhetoric, but a rather sober assessment of the current state of politics in Scotland and the need to ensure that the defeat of independence didn't lead to a period of introversion and negativity. She called for a 'progressive alliance' with other parties in the rest of the UK to promote social democratic policies.

But though her delivery was rather less dramatic than the surroundings, the 2015 SNP manifesto was to generate a furious reaction in the press. It offered a 0.5% increase in investment spending over five years, a mansion tax, restoration of the 50p tax band, an end to the bedroom tax and the introduction of what Sturgeon now called 'full fiscal responsibility' for Holyrood. The leader of the Scottish National Party hardly mentioned independence, let alone a second referendum which she said would only happen after a 'material change' in circumstances. Though, under questioning, she was vague about what that material change might be.

She promised Scottish voters that under the SNP 'Scotland's voice would be heard loud and clear in Westminster', but her main audience was the UK. Wearing one of her trademark vivid red dresses, Sturgeon promised to work 'responsibly and constructively' with Labour and other parties in Westminster to lock the Conservatives out of government. This moderate tone contrasted sharply with the noises emanating from Westminster. That very morning, the London Mayor Boris Johnson had compared the First Minister to King Herod, Lady Macbeth, and a 'voracious weevil' – all in the same article.[43] The Prime Minister, David Cameron, had described the 'frightening' prospect of SNP involvement in the government of the UK and said a Miliband/Sturgeon alliance would be a 'match made in hell'.[44]

The journalists in the arena probably hoped there would be a response in kind. Would she hurl one of those huge rocks at Boris? But they were to be disappointed. Ms Sturgeon simply noted that the mayor's remarks had been 'entirely offensive', and moved on. There were no histrionics, no claims of 'jockophobia' or anti-Scottish bigotry. She didn't even try to fire jokes at her detractors. The First Minister argued that it was unacceptable in a democracy for David Cameron to suggest – as he had that weekend – that it was only 'legitimate' for Scottish MPs to sit in Westminster provided they voted the way he wanted them to.

How different from her predecessor Alex Salmond. He relished confrontation and verbal swordplay with the press and Westminster politicians. You can imagine the kind of thing Salmond might have said: 'Who is Bullingdon Boris to lecture us on democracy when his Eton chums rule Scotland despite having fewer MPs in Scotland than giant pandas in Edinburgh Zoo'. Or something like that. But the former First Minister was significant in the climbing arena only by his absence. This was the emergence onto a national stage of a new force in British politics, a powerful female politician who seems to regard adversarial banter as rather pointless.

Of course, Scotland already knew all about Nicola Sturgeon, having seen her perform in office as Deputy First Minister since 2007 and First Minister since October 2014. But for the UK press, whose image of the SNP is inextricably bound up with the rotund silhouette of Alex Salmond, this was something of an election campaign bombshell. The UK correspondents were mostly star-struck and she received rave reviews all round: 'powerful', 'assured', 'confident'. 'Nicola rocks', said one observer. There was much talk about how impressive she looked, though most correspondents avoided too much reference to her physical appearance for fear of appearing in #everydaysexism.

Much more important than her fluent performance or her high heels, Nicola Sturgeon established herself that day as a leading spokesperson of the British Left. No one had heard a senior elected political leader articulate socialist politics this forthrightly since the days of Tony Benn, with whom Nicola Sturgeon was subsequently compared (ironically, since he was a lifelong opponent of nationalism and devolution). Though what made it more significant than leftist rhetoric was that Ms Sturgeon had actually been serving minister and putting these principles into practice for nearly eight years.

Some say that the SNP is far less radical in government than it claims to be, and that may be true. She believes the SNP's record on defending universal benefits, promoting the living wage, opposing Trident and austerity economics speaks for itself. It was Nicola Sturgeon who brought to an end private sector provision in the Scottish NHS in 2008. Scots, however, have had time to become sceptical about the SNP's radical left rhetoric now that it is the party of government in Scotland. But for a UK audience used to the narrow confines of the Lib/Lab/Tory single transferrable ideology, this was something new. Unilateral nuclear disarmament, for example, is a policy that has been off the Westminster agenda now for a quarter of a century.

Not everyone was enamoured of the 'Sturgeonator', however. The former editor of the left-wing *Mirror*, Piers Morgan, described the First Minister as 'a diminutive but sharp-witted woman who has rampaged through the UK election campaign like a mini-Godzilla breathing fire and brimstone'. *The Sun* columnist Trevor Kavanagh said: 'Nicola Sturgeon may wear high heels and a short skirt, but she eats her partners alive.' *The Daily Mail* said of her performance: 'Even by her own megalomaniac standards, Nicola Sturgeon's language on the day of her manifesto launch is breathtaking in its arrogance.' The next day the *Daily Mail* headlined a front page splash on the SNP manifesto with a picture of the First Minister and the words: 'How I'll blackmail England for £148 billion by the most dangerous woman in Britain.' She said it was 'the nicest thing they've ever said about me'. The *Sun* had earlier caused controversy by depicting Ms Sturgeon in a tartan bikini sitting on a wrecking ball. Even the *Times* front page said the First Minister was 'holding the UK to ransom'.

Female columnists objected that the condemnation of the SNP verged on sexism.[45] But this withering scorn from the UK press only seemed to enhance the First Minister's appeal in Scotland.

Sturgeon is intelligent, of course, but more than that she has a self-confidence which few female politicians possess in a political world which is still largely male dominated. And she wears her learning lightly. Working class intellectuals are prone to pomposity – Roy Hattersley comes to mind – and political leaders often like to show off or bully people with their cleverness. But Nicola Sturgeon never seems to need to prove her intellect. After decades working and campaigning in working class Glasgow she has acquired an ability to express complex ideas in down-to-earth language that anyone can understand. And as she demonstrated in the Climbing Arena, this sure-footed politician isn't easily provoked.

THE MUNT

I remember Nicola Sturgeon as a rather solemn and dowdy young woman who used to come up to me at party conferences when I was BBC political presenter years ago to complain about my slant on things. And she may have had a point. The BBC has always tended to take its agenda – at least in the priority it gives certain stories – from the press, and in the late 1990s, the press was even more virulently hostile to the SNP than it is today. But while she was clearly intelligent and someone to be reckoned with, I never thought then that Ms Sturgeon would go on to become leader of the party, still less that she would emerge into the limelight as the political star she is today. More fool me. Yet, most people in the politics profession remember her as a politician who was never over-generous with her smiles. That reputation as a 'nippy sweetie' for most meant that she was a little hard-bitten and spiky.[46]

Nicola Sturgeon isn't a great public speaker in the conventional sense – she doesn't really do ridicule or emotion – but she conveys a sense of authenticity and honesty that people respect. She gives the impression that she understands ordinary people's lives. She seems approachable, natural, and friendly, and has a unique rapport with her public – especially the swarms of women who approach her for selfies after events. She was heard to remark after one such event that she didn't know how politicians did campaigns before camera phones were invented. No one does selfies like Nicola Sturgeon and it has projected her smiling face across the front pages of every newspaper in Scotland.

Most politicians reveal the burdens of office in the bags under their eyes. Nicola Sturgeon seems to positively enjoy it. Friends testify that she seems to have found herself in leadership and thrives on the challenges, the physical and mental demands of office. Certainly she has never looked happier or more relaxed than she did in the heat of the 2015 General Election campaign, as the First Minister of Scotland, working 24/7 for the cause of independence. This is unlike so many ministers and senior male politicians I've spoken to in the past who often claim to find the strain of office almost unbearable. Perhaps some women just cope better than men with the multiple and conflicting demands of statecraft.

Female politicians often submit to the indignity of being surrounded by style consultants and voice coaches who succeed only in making them look unnatural and false. Somehow Nicola Sturgeon has avoided all that, though she did admit on ITV's Loose Women that she had once been given voice coaching by Sean Connery.[47] The First Minister also said that being in the public eye gave her an opportunity to promote Scottish fashion designers like Edinburgh-based Totty Rocks. She always looks well turned out without appearing to be fashion conscious or dressing to impress any particular demographic. She accepts that people will talk about her appearance but she manages not to be diminished by it. Nicola Sturgeon uses her personality to promote her social democratic politics; she doesn't let it get in the way.

This Red Queen is of course, first and foremost, a nationalist, and has been since she joined the Scottish National Party at the age of sixteen when she attended Greenwood Academy in Irvine, twenty-five miles southwest of Glasgow. She was born there in 1970 and grew up in the unglamorous-sounding village of Dreghorn two miles outside Irvine with her parents Robin, an electrician, Joan, a dental nurse, and her sister Gillian. She was educated at the local school, hung around bus shelters, and allegedly used to take boyfriends up the 'Munt' or the Mount – a hill in Dreghorn – as recreation.[48] Nothing at this stage, except her voracious reading, suggested that this Irvine lass was destined to be Britain's most popular politician, according to some opinion polls, and 'Britain's most dangerous woman' according to the *Daily Mail*.

There is frustratingly little written about Nicola Sturgeon's early life. There is only one biography, an unauthorised one from the Scottish journalist David Torrance, to whom she refused to speak. If her background is sketchy, she says it's because there isn't much to say. When asked once by Frankie Boyle what she would say to her sixteen-year-old self, Sturgeon is supposed to have replied: 'Lighten up…and then the girl of sixteen would say eff off.'[49] I can't think of any other politician of comparable standing anywhere in Europe about whom so little is known.

If most articles about Nicola Sturgeon tend to read like hagiographies then it is partly because there are remarkably few negative stories about her. Frustrated Labour Peers like George Foulkes have taken to calling her 'Saint Nicola' and suggest that journalists are reluctant to criticise her or investigate her dark side. But there seems little to find out. She is a career politician, married to a career politician, the SNP

Chief Executive Peter Murrell since 2010. They do politics. He cooks. The only known scandal that emerged during Nicola Sturgeon's ministerial career involved a constituent on whose behalf she wrote a letter to a court in 2010. The former Deputy First Minister had to apologise to parliament for lobbying the judge to give Abdul Rauf a non-custodial sentence after he admitted an £80,000 benefits fraud. He said they were mistakes. The incident led to calls for her resignation, but she weathered the storm.[50]

During the General Election campaign you can be sure that every tabloid journalist in the land was on the hunt for stories about Nicola Sturgeon. The worst that the *Sun* could come up with was that she had once sheared the hair of her sister Gillian's Barbie doll. 'It was an early sign,' the paper claimed, 'of the ruthlessness of the woman who would split up the UK.'[51] This dark tale was illustrated with a then-and-now picture montage of Sturgeon under the banner 'Scotweiler'. In mock seriousness, the First Minister responded to the story by tweeting to a follower that, 'I'm not proud of it, Linda, but I've changed. My niece's dolls have never come to any harm'. She went on to remark that the *Sun* had got it wrong; her sister Gillian's doll was not a Barbie but a Sindy. Later, nationalists on Twitter started posting images of mutilated dolls and within hours #dollgate was trending No.1 across the entire UK.

Irvine, where the doll-mutilator was brought up, was a postwar new town built on top of one of Scotland's ancient capitals. It was a product of enlightened postwar social planning, intended to provide a new future for the industrial working class. And for many years it provided secure employment and a high standard of social housing. But its salad days were brief. Built on light engineering, it was vulnerable to recession. Irvine turned into something of an urban wasteland after it suffered the ravages of the 1980s industrial clearances wrought by monetarist experiments of early Thatcherism.

It wasn't romantic Scottish nationalism or even intense

patriotism that turned Nicola Sturgeon to the Scottish National Party. It was experience of unemployment and economic insecurity in her neighbourhood. When Alex Salmond talks of his early political beliefs he talks of how his grandfather used to tell him stories from Scottish history: the wars of independence, Stirling Bridge, Bannockburn. For Nicola Sturgeon, it was the Proclaimers. The Scottish pop duo's hit single 'Letter from America' (1987) cited Irvine as one of the many Scottish industrial areas that had been ravaged by the recessions of the 1980s: 'Bathgate no more; Linwood no more; Irvine no more.' She played it constantly. Her essentially socialist consciousness was overlaid with a profound sense of grievance that her country was being ruled, not so much by a foreign power, as by a foreign ideology: British Conservatism. 'Thatcher was the motivation of my entire political career. I hated everything she stood for.'[52]

She went on to study law at Glasgow University where she acquired many of her debating skills as a student nationalist. After graduation she became a solicitor and later worked in Drumchapel Law Centre, in the Glasgow suburb famously described by the comedian Billy Connolly as 'a desert wi' windaes'. There she dealt with the broken lives of the casualties of post-industrial Scotland and saw the human potential that was being wasted. Her direct experience of social disorganisation in this vast housing scheme convinced her that Scotland needed to undergo a national transformation if it was to escape from its dependency culture. Nicola Sturgeon is not a follower of the former Tory leader and welfare reformer Iain Duncan Smith, who made those infamous visits to Glasgow's Easterhouse estate a decade ago. But she does believe that people need to be inspired to develop their own potential. As she said in her inaugural speech as Scotland's first female First Minister: 'There should be no limit to your ambition or what you can achieve. If you are good enough and if you work hard enough, the sky is the limit.'[53]

Scottish politics is intensely tribal, and being in the wrong party in those days meant accepting that many areas of work, in the public sector, media, and local government, were pretty well off limits to SNP activists. It's not entirely clear whether Nicola Sturgeon dreamed of a brilliant career in the law because her sights were always fixed firmly on a political career. At the age of twenty-one she was the youngest candidate in the 1992 General Election, standing for Glasgow Shettleston. She lost by 15,000 votes. She spent most of the next decade losing elections until she eventually became the list MSP for the Glasgow region in the Scottish Parliament after it was reconvened in 1999.

Thereafter she rose swiftly through the ministerial ranks becoming one of the main challengers for the SNP leadership in 2004 when over-promoted John Swinney resigned. It was then that she struck the so-called 'deal' with Alex Salmond in the Champney Inn near Linlithgow to stand down and allow him a clear run as SNP leader.[54] He had returned from a three year 'sabbatical' in Westminster. This arrangement worked rather better than the infamous Granita deal between Tony Blair and Gordon Brown in 1994, which led to the two most powerful figures in the Labour Party spending nearly a decade at each other's throats. Alex Salmond delivered and she became Deputy First Minister in the first SNP administration in Holyrood in 2007.

She also acquired the onerous post of Health Secretary – often a graveyard of political careers. But not in her case. Episodes like the international swine flu epidemic demonstrated her competence and communication skills. She managed to negotiate six years in charge of the biggest and most demanding brief in the Scottish cabinet. Her reward after the 2011 SNP election landslide was to be given the even more onerous responsibility of winning what looked like an unwinnable referendum on independence as Constitution Secretary. The 'Yes Minister' as she was called played a major role in drafting the 2013 independence White Paper *Scotland's Future*. If this sounded more like a social democratic election manifesto than a declaration of independence, that was largely because of Nicola Sturgeon's influence. The emphasis throughout was on social justice and equality. The 'big idea' in the White Paper was a pledge to introduce free childcare to 'liberate' 100,000 Scottish women to go into the workplace.

William Wallace and Robert the Bruce were singularly absent from the independence White Paper and I can honestly say I have never heard Nicola Sturgeon mention the heroes of Scottish independence. She seems uninterested in emotional Bannockburn nationalism and often sounds less overtly patriotic than her political opponents. The former Scottish Labour leader, Jim Murphy, seemed forever to be proclaiming his Scottishness. The former Labour Prime Minister Gordon Brown's book *My Scotland Our Britain* begins with the words: 'I love my country. Simple as that. I am passionately and proudly Scottish,' and then goes on to gush about football and Robert Burns. I'm sure Nicola Sturgeon loves her country too, but you very rarely hear her using that kind of rhetoric. She seems much more passionate about gender equality than about national identity.

What she is absolutely single-minded about is power. She bided her time as Alex Salmond's deputy but made clear during the 2014 referendum campaign that she was his rightful successor. And when Salmond announced his resignation on the day after the referendum defeat, there was never any doubt that she would become SNP leader and First Minister of Scotland. This was a coronation rather than a leadership contest. She has never been elected to either post. But no one seemed to feel that this undermined her authority or her legitimacy. Nicola Sturgeon was so obviously the best person for the job that a contest would have seemed pointless. However, her dominance of her party is something that makes the opposition parties distinctly uneasy and has led to talk of 'a sinister centralism' in the Scottish government.[55]

Once installed in the official residence at Bute House in Edinburgh, she moved rapidly to introduce a gender-balanced cabinet, one of only three in such governments in Europe. She pledged to eliminate the pay gap in public sector employment, combat domestic violence, and extend free childcare. She said her ambition was to make Scotland 'a prosperous and fair nation', which showed that Nicola Sturgeon is just as prone to empty clichés as any of her political contemporaries. The Scottish Parliament is unique in that the three most powerful figures in it are women. Sturgeon offered to work constructively with the Scottish Tory leader, Ruth Davidson, and Labour's parliamentary leader, Kezia Dugdale. The sisterly solidarity lasted all of a week.

Dugdale has been tenacious in her challenges to the First Minister. Before long Sturgeon was finding herself under sustained pressure over breaking her own party's pledges on waiting times in Accident and Emergency. The 'reckless' policy of full fiscal autonomy was also subjected to withering scrutiny by Labour, especially after the collapse of oil prices in December 2014. 'It's clear that when the numbers don't add up, this First Minister makes them up anyway,' was typical of the attacks from deputy leader Dugdale (the then Scottish Labour leader Jim Murphy was an MP in Westminster and did not appear at question time in Holyrood). If the SNP has indeed backtracked on full fiscal autonomy, as many believe, then much of the credit for that must go to Kezia Dugdale.[56]

Perhaps the most serious political challenge faced by Sturgeon in the months after she became First Minister was over Police Scotland. In 2014 under its headstrong Chief Constable Sir Stephen House, the newly-merged Scottish police force had started to behave in an extremely odd way. Armed police started appearing on the streets, in shopping centres, and at routine incidents in the Highlands and the Borders. It emerged that Stop and Search was taking place on an apparently indiscriminate basis, and that Scots were four times more likely to be frisked than citizens in London. 'Consensual' Stop and Search was also taking place with children under 12 years of age. There were criticisms from figures like the Advocate General, Lord Wallace, that Sir Stephen had 'too much power'. When confronted with this Sir Stephen did not convince his inquisitors at the Holyrood Justice Committee.[57] Liberals and civil rights activists were disappointed when Nicola Sturgeon expressed her 'full confidence' in Sir Stephen. There has been concern among even some who are sympathetic to the SNP that there is a danger of Scotland becoming 'a police state' under her watch.[58]

However, the affair seemed to do her little damage in the country. The constitutional debate has so dominated Scottish politics over recent years that it is difficult for rival issues to get traction – something that also worries those of us who fear that even the best governments can get up to no good when they are not under public scrutiny.

@NICOLA TWEETS

The General Election campaign had hardly started when on April 3rd the *Daily Telegraph*'s Scottish political editor, Simon Johnson, announced that he had an exclusive story in the next day's paper. He had received a leaked Foreign Office memo in which it was claimed that the First Minister had told the French Ambassador, Sylvie Bermann, that the Labour leader Ed Miliband was 'not Prime Ministerial material' and that 'she'd rather see David Cameron remain Prime Minister'. This was potentially hugely damaging to the First Minister. She had insisted that she would never support the Conservatives or help David Cameron into government. 'It's deja vu all over again,' said the Scottish Labour leader Jim Murphy, 'the SNP say one thing in public but another in private.'[59]

At 9.43pm Sturgeon tweeted '@simonjohnson your story is categorically, 100% untrue... which I'd have told you if you'd asked me at any point today.'This is the kind of off-the-cuff response that horrifies senior civil servants and political advisers. Had she checked? Was it 'categorically' untrue or just mainly untrue? Had the paper tried to contact anyone in the Scottish Government machine? In the event, her smart response pretty much killed the *Daily Telegraph* story stone dead. Her categorical rebuttal, combined with the failure of the journalist to have contacted the First Minister for a comment prior to publication, frightened off most of the rest of the media – though the BBC was still headlining Sturgeon 'denying' the story the next morning. The French Ambassador Sylvie Bermann later denied that she had said what was in the memo, which appeared to have been confused in translation anyway.

Rarely has a story rebounded on its perpetrators so rapidly. Within twenty-four hours Twitter was alive with rumours that the leak had come from the Scottish Office. The Scottish Secretary at the time, the Liberal Democrat Alistair Carmichael, said he had not heard of the leak until a journalist told him about it and remarked 'these things happen in elections'. An inquiry was initiated by the Cabinet Secretary, Sir Jeremy Heywood. Only after polling day did Carmichael admit that he had authorised the leak to the *Daily Telegraph* and had lied about not knowing about its content. This provoked a storm of criticism, calls for Carmichael's resignation, and an action in the Court of Session to overturn his election victory in Orkney and Shetland. It was a story that did not end well.[60]

Nicola Sturgeon is one of the first elected national leaders ever to appear as herself on Twitter on a daily basis. Most politicians allow media advisers and press officers to handle their social media accounts along with the rest of their PR. But with 'Nicola' what you see really is what you get. Sturgeon's aides worry about the risks she takes issuing remarks in real time. But so far her appearances on social media have been very effective, not just in teasing the *Sun* and rounding on sexist comments, but at killing negative stories.

Nicola Sturgeon has also used Twitter to present a much more rounded picture of herself than could ever come over in official pronouncements and speeches. She is human; she is real. The First Minister even has a genuine sense of humour. During a row in March 2015 about Ed Miliband having two kitchens in his Islington home, I tweeted a picture of a younger Nicola Sturgeon in a kitchen and asked why similar attention hadn't been paid to her kitchens. 'Scotland – always ignored.' She replied: 'All questions about my kitchen should be directed to @petermurrell [her husband] – he is better acquainted with it than I am.'

Now, this exchange was remarkable in a number of respects. First of all, it is not long ago that female politicians were required to demonstrate their domestic skills in the most humiliating manner. Remember the footage of Margaret Thatcher cooking her husband Denis' breakfast in Number Ten? Clearly, we are now in a new political age in which female politicians need not prove their competence at baking cookies. The First Minister's Twitter feed has also filled the gap left by the lack of biographical knowledge about her. She has used it to confirm to her huge number of admirers that she is a genuine person and not just a political construct.

Of course, politicians who get involved in Twitter also run the risk being accused of lacking seriousness and even demeaning their office. Indeed, referring to my exchange with the First Minister, the *Daily Mail* took her to task for 'tweeting jokes about her kitchen' on a day when she could have been attending a memorial service in St Paul's Cathedral in London for Afghan war dead. Bereaved families of the 38 Scots who died in the conflict were quoted as saying her behaviour was an 'insult' to their loved ones.[61]

But Nicola Sturgeon doesn't just use Twitter for jokes. The previous month on Twitter I had criticised her decision to end the automatic right of early release for criminals serving life sentences. I said it was illiberal. She immediately responded saying it wasn't and a discussion ensued on Twitter. I was, as some others tweeted in Scottish parlance, 'telt' by the First Minister. It is disconcerting, to say the least, to be pontificating on Twitter one minute and the next to find yourself suddenly speaking to the country's top politicians. Being 'Sturgeoned' on social media is certainly exhilarating and brings a new dimension to political journalism. I'm not sure, however, that it is such a good idea for politicians to be getting this closely involved. There are pitfalls – predictive text can sometimes mangle replies. There are now Sturgeon parody accounts on the Internet that could cause mischief. But it is a sign of Sturgeon's extraordinary political self-confidence that she never seems to be concerned about how her tweets might be misconstrued. As in television interviews, she seems to know exactly what she wants to say, and says it.

It is in this directness that Nicola Sturgeon demonstrates her modernity. She is not surrounded by advisers and there is no glass wall or mystique of power between her and her public. It is very hard to do this convincingly unless you really do it yourself. Reading the Labour leadership candidate Liz Kendal's obviously manufactured twitter feed @lizforleader is like listening to a speak-your-weight machine by comparison (e.g. Liz: 'we must be the champion of every child and passionate about ensuring they get the life chances they deserve'). To do social media effectively, politicians must above all convey authenticity and sound real. Nicola Sturgeon does.

'So what makes Sturgeon so dangerous?' asked the columnist Deborah Orr in the *Guardian*.[62] 'It's because she's a great politician. But it's also because she's an authentic politician [...] What Sturgeon has is clarity.' The fact that she does this while being leader of her party and the country exposes her to unusual risks. It is a heroic effort at openness, never attempted before at this level, which could end in disaster. She has spin-doctors, of course, but the one thing no one can say about Nicola Sturgeon is that she is reliant on them.

UTILITARIAN NATIONALISM

There is little doubt that Nicola Sturgeon's use of social media has contributed to her extraordinary popularity. But what made an even greater impact during the 2015 General Election was her performance in the live televised debates. Almost from the moment she stepped onto the stage for the BBC's seven-way leadership debate on 16th April, Sturgeon became the star turn. She spoke clearly and with conviction, continuing her anti-austerity alliance theme, condemning weapons of mass destruction and insisting that she would make Ed Miliband 'bolder' in government. By the time she and the two other female leaders, Leanne Wood of Plaid Cymru and Natalie Bennett of the Greens, had their famous group hug, the 'Queen of Scotland' had won over even the most critical tabloids.[63]

Most opinion polls, even in the UK, said that the SNP leader had won the debate. Her personal popularity, already high, rocketed and by 21st April, You Gov had her net approval rating as plus 42, against her main rival, Jim Murphy, on minus 22, Cameron minus 30, and Ed Miliband on minus 31. Indeed, a *TNS/Herald* survey concluded that Sturgeon was 'the most popular politician, not just in Scotland, but in the UK'.[64] This made very little obvious sense, since at that very moment the Conservatives were successfully attacking Ed Miliband for contemplating a deal with 'the most dangerous woman'. Somehow, many English voters managed to be impressed by Nicola Sturgeon at the same time as feeling threatened by her party.

Her party's popularity in Scotland went from the heady to the ridiculous. The SNP entered the campaign in March with a solid lead over Labour, but after Nicola's appearance in the first UK televised debate they went ballistic. By 17th April, the *Times/TNS* poll had the SNP at 52%, Labour at 24%, Scottish Conservatives at 13%, Scottish Liberal Democrats on 6%, and the Scottish Green Party on 3%. I tweeted: 'Blow for Sturgeon as nearly half of Scots say they plan NOT to vote for SNP'. It was meant to be a joke, but irony is very dangerous on Twitter, and a number of people thought I was serious. The Labour-supporting commentator, Dan Hodges, tweeted that the figures were 'insane'. And they were.

There is no doubt that the SNP's huge popularity is largely down to Nicola Sturgeon. But it would be facile to suggest that her personality alone was responsible for this; her anti-austerity message also clearly resonates, at least with voters in Scotland. What she conspicuously avoided was any flag-waging Scottish chauvinism. There was no emotional or romantic nationalism in her appeal to the nation in her TV debates. She does not trade on anti-English sentiment and is fierce with supporters on the Internet who use 'quisling', 'traitor', or other divisive nationalist language. Nicola Sturgeon famously describes herself as a 'utilitarian nationalist' as opposed to an 'existential nationalist'. By this, she means that she is interested first of all in social justice, and that national independence is really just a means to achieving social democratic ends. On social media, as everywhere else, Nicola Sturgeon presents herself as a pragmatic left-wing politician who just happens to be leading a nationalist party. You get the impression that she could just as easily be leading a left-wing Labour Party as the Scottish National Party. Indeed, a former Labour official put it to me during the campaign that Nicola Sturgeon was the best leader Labour never had.

Most nationalist parties in Europe, like the French National Front or the True Finns, are either based on ethnic exceptionalism, anti-immigration, cultural chauvinism, or resistance to foreign domination. Nicola Sturgeon genuinely abhors this kind of narrow nationalism. Her speeches invariably call for a 'progressive alliance' with other social democratic parties. There is an obvious contradiction here. Her SNP followers like to pour hatred on the 'Red Tory Scum' in the Labour Party, but here she was at the 2015 General Election offering to help the scum get into government. Some of her supporters in the '45' nationalist sector of SNP support must have wondered why, after all these years of condemning Labour, they were being told that they had to support them. For many SNP members, Labour are like the Tories, only worse. They are collaborators with the Westminster establishment, not potential allies in the struggle for national freedom.

However, this contradiction – if such it is – between social democrat and nationalist didn't appear to bother most supporters during the campaign or after it. There has been no obvious dissent in the ranks of the SNP as there was twenty years ago when Alex Salmond threw the party behind Labour's devolution and antagonised the so-called 'fundamentalists' in his party. The membership seems content to support Sturgeon whatever their leader does, so long as it furthers the cause of independence. And like Salmond, Nicola Sturgeon has certainly done that.

There has been much speculation in the press that she and Alex Salmond are heading for a confrontation, essentially because she is much less of an old-style nationalist than he is. Alex Salmond has been accused of briefing the press in Westminster about an early independence referendum, which Nicola Sturgeon does not want.[65] It is hard to imagine Alex Salmond settling down quietly on the back benches at Westminster as an elder statesman. He can't help making news wherever he goes. He likes the company of journalists much more than Nicola Sturgeon does. She rarely spends time drinking and talking with them late at night, as Salmond has been so known to do. This is a difference of personality more than politics, but it could clearly pose difficulties in future and there is certainly the potential for a north-south divide between the forceful foreign affairs spokesman in Westminster and the First Minister in Holyrood.

However, I do not believe that there is as yet any significant split emerging in the leadership of the SNP. This is mainly because Nicola Sturgeon's authority in the party, a result of her extraordinary electoral success, is so great it is difficult to imagine any such challenge succeeding, certainly not from Alex Salmond. There is no one else in the party, as yet, who is showing signs of leadership ambitions. The sense everyone in the party gets is that Nicola Sturgeon remains very much in control. But there is always going to be a question mark over her attitude and determination to achieve full national independence. Nicola Sturgeon has made it clear she is in no hurry to call another referendum, and her suggestion that all the 'family of nations' should have a veto on the decision on British membership of Europe has led some to conclude that she is essentially now a supporter of federalism and not separation from the UK. The former SNP leader, Gordon Wilson, believes that 'independence has been 'sidelined' and that the SNP 'is moving away from Scottish independence towards British federalism'.[66] The First Minister insists this is not the case, but it is clear that the Scottish National Party under Nicola Sturgeon is less 'nationalist' than it has ever been in its eighty year history.

It is therefore ironic that she could very well be the political leader who leads Scotland to independence as a result of Scotland's electoral revolution. No one should underestimate her determination to achieve this objective. The First Minister's nationalism may be utilitarian but that doesn't mean it is optional. It is the misfortune of the UK to find itself faced with a national leader of this stature at this critical moment in its history. Everything Nicola Sturgeon does from here on will be dedicated to ensuring that the Union's crisis is truly existential.

Chapter Four:

New Jim

On December 13th 2014, the Scottish Labour Party was hit by a hurricane. It was picked up by the scruff of the neck, hurled round and round until it no longer knew which way was up, and then hurled into a general election it couldn't hope to win. It may never recover from the shock. The hurricane in question was called Jim Murphy and he plunged the Scottish Labour Party into six months of organisational, ideological, constitutional and emotional turmoil.

He has also now presided over Labour's worst ever electoral defeat and the loss of all but one of its Scottish MPs. And even after his departure as leader, he left the party fighting in the ruins by appearing to blame not himself, but Unite's Len McCluskey, for Labour's Scottish woes on the grounds that the union leader was too influential in the party.[67] There is now a debate about whether or not Labour in Scotland should set itself up as a separate party from UK Labour, a move which one former Scottish MP, Tom Harris, said would cause him to leave the party altogether.[68] Jim Murphy is a decent and personable man, but history will not be kind to him as a political leader.

Admittedly, when the former UK Labour minister took over something drastic needed to be done. The Scottish Labour Party that had dominated the Scottish political landscape in the 1980s and 90s, sending up to 56 MPs to Westminster in 1997, was in a sorry state. Its membership had dwindled to little more than 10,000. It was out of power and out of luck. Murphy tried to reposition it initially to the left of the SNP, trying to outflank it on wealth taxes and on increased NHS spending. But he ended up revisiting the mistakes made by the Better Together campaign in the 2014 referendum. Jim Murphy is justified in saying that he was not the sole cause of the collapse of the Scottish Labour Party, though he undoubtedly made things worse. Labour's problems were deep-seated and profound and it is worth taking some time to reflect on where they came from, if only to understand where Labour must go from here.

A MUDDLE NOT A FIDDLE

The party that had delivered Scottish devolution and restored the Scottish Parliament after 300 years in 1999, under the popular First Minister Donald Dewar, did not thrive in Holyrood's political environment. The lacklustre, accident-prone, and apparently corrupt leadership of Dewar's successors fatally undermined Labour's image during the chaotic early years of devolution. The resignation of the Labour First Minister Henry McLeish in 2001 over the subletting of his constituency offices may have been more comic opera than corruption – he called it 'a muddle not a fiddle' – but it looked very bad. Labour seemed dogged by scandals like the 'lobbygate' allegations of cash-for-access. The resignation in 2008 of its most intelligent and capable leader, Wendy Alexander, over an unlawful campaign donation sealed the impression of a party riven, if not by actual wrong-doing, then by self-destructive factionalism and incompetence.

But it was a combination of the Iraq War and Tony Blair's reforms to the welfare state that really damaged Labour in Scotland. The invasion of Baghdad was widely opposed in Scotland after 2003. The introduction of university tuition fees and then top-up fees in 2004 – reneging on promises made in successive Labour election manifestos – offended social democratic sentiment in Scotland. As did the moves by the UK Labour government to end what Tony Blair called 'monopoly state provision' in public services, especially the National Health Service. Tony Blair's enthusiasm for renewing the Trident weapons of mass destruction on the Clyde was another negative.

By 2007, the SNP had managed to get a toehold on power in Holyrood by stealing Labour's social democratic clothing and capitalising on Tony Blair's unpopularity. It has often been remarked that in May 2007 Labour needn't have relinquished power. Salmond only had a one vote advantage and relied on the tacit support of the Tory leader Annabel Goldie to become First Minister and get his early budgets passed. Just as in Westminster there is no rule that the largest party has to be the government in Holyrood if it doesn't have an overall majority. However, at the time, the Liberal Democrat-Labour coalition simply lacked the will to 'lock the nationalists out' and carry on.

Once they got their feet under the table, the energetic SNP ministers drove the Scottish Executive as never before. Their enthusiasm and imaginative minority government was a huge presentational success, as even Nicola Sturgeon herself admits.[69] The Nationalists consolidated their position as social democratic champions by defending universal benefits like free personal care, rejecting market reforms in the NHS, and introducing crowd-pleasing measures like the abolition of prescription charges.

Labour didn't get the message, however, and by 2011, under another underpowered leader in Iain Gray, the party plunged to disaster in a general election campaign defined by amateurism, opportunism, cynicism, and bathos. Incredible to relate, Labour entered the Scottish parliamentary election campaign in April 2011 with a 10 point opinion poll lead over the SNP; it ended by losing to Alex Salmond by the same margin. The hounding of Gray into a Subway sandwich bar by anti-cuts protesters seemed to confirm the image of a party on the run.[70]

The map of Scotland turned SNP yellow overnight. Former Labour ministers like Margaret Curran lost their seats – an experience that Ms Curran was to revisit in 2015 as she lost the safe Westminster seat in Glasgow she had been given as a consolation. And what was particularly galling to many in the shattered Scottish Labour Party was the knowledge that the SNP had largely won its landslide on the basis of the policies Labour had rejected. The SNP manifesto was a résumé of the kind of social democratic politics that the Labour Party used to favour such as free higher education. 'Rocks will melt in the sun' said Alex Salmond, before the SNP would reintroduce tuition fees. Free personal care for the elderly had actually been introduced by the Lib-Lab coalition in 2001, yet somehow it became identified with the SNP.

The SNP never expected to win an absolute majority in 2011 – most believed that under the additional member voting system this was almost impossible in Holyrood. But they did, and that triggered the 2014 independence referendum. The Prime Minister David Cameron, who believed the risk of Scots voting for independence to be very minor, agreed to legitimise a single question – Yes or No – referendum under the Edinburgh Agreement of 2012.

At first, Labour believed that this constitutional event could be their liberation. There seemed no prospect of Alex Salmond actually winning a referendum since only around 30% of Scots said they wanted formal independence. The vast majority always said – and continue to say – that they wanted a Scottish parliament with economic powers usually called 'devo max'. Labour hoped that a defeated Alex Salmond would be driven from politics and that Labour would be restored to favour as the champions of non-separatist home rule. They were half right.

The Better Together campaign did win the independence referendum, by a comfortable margin of 55% to 45%, and Salmond resigned immediately. But then something remarkable happened. The Scottish voters seemed to embrace nationalism as never before. By handing over to his deputy, Nicola Sturgeon, Salmond drew a line under the lost election, and proclaimed instead that the 1.6 million Scots who voted Yes were the moral victors. Sturgeon proceeded to hold a series of barnstorming speaking engagements across Scotland, for all the world as if the SNP had won the referendum rather than lost it.

Other groups energised by the referendum also carried on as if nothing had happened. The Radical Independence Campaign – an alliance of far left and green groups – held a rally in November 2014 attended by an unprecedented 3,000 people. The organisation Women for Independence also kept on keeping on and convened gatherings of up to 1000 strong. But it was the SNP which benefited to the greatest degree from the referendum effect and, by the New Year, its membership had nearly quadrupled to 105,000. This made the SNP the third largest party in the entire UK after Labour and the Conservatives.

But worse was to come for the stunned Scottish Labour Party. Disgusted at the aftermath and the conduct of the Better Together campaign, the Scottish Labour leader Johann Lamont resigned in high drama in October 2014 claiming that she had been ill-treated by the Labour leadership in London.[71] She said that London Labour regarded the Scottish party as little more than a 'branch office'. Worse, she condemned some of her former colleagues on the Labour benches in Westminster as 'dinosaurs'. This was deeply shocking to many in the party, not because Lamont resigned – she was never a very strong leader – but because she had used the kind of language that had been used for years by the SNP to attack the Scottish Labour Party.

This brought to a head an ideological crisis about the nature and viability of the welfare state that had been developing within Labour over the previous twenty years. When Lamont had taken over as leader from the hapless Iain Gray in the wake of the 2011 rout, she had made two significant policy initiatives. She set up a commission to investigate the prospects for further devolution to Holyrood, and she invited academics, like the public finance expert Professor Arthur Midwinter, to review the affordability of universal benefits, such as free care for the elderly, concessionary bus fares and university tuition fees. She described these in a speech in Edinburgh's Hub in December 2012 as aspects of a 'something for nothing society'.[72]

She was reflecting, in part, on the attitudes of the Blairite ascendancy in Westminster, which was opposed to universalism in areas such as higher education. The Chancellor Gordon Brown had departed from the old Labour principles of the welfare state in favour of benefits that were in his words 'targeted' specifically at low income groups. Lamont was also speaking for a significant number in the Scottish party who believed that the benefits Alex Salmond called the 'social wage', were not socialist at all, but were an electoral bribe to the Scottish middle classes. Why, they said, should poorer workers pay, through their taxes, for free tuition for middle class children? Why should elderly people, living in valuable homes with significant equity, have their personal care subsidised by the less well off? Some called the SNP's programme of free bridge tolls, free hospital parking, and free prescriptions the 'free stuff'.

Universalism – especially in education and health – had of course been a foundation of the welfare state introduced by Labour after the Second World War. It had then been argued that the middle classes needed to have a stake in the system if they were to contribute to paying for state provision through their taxes. Also, the memory of the means test in the 1930s persuaded most social democrats after the war that education, health, and social security should be paid for out of general taxation to avoid stigma and also to avoid the bureaucratic costs of targeting services to the less well off. But by the 1990s, many 'modernisers' in the Labour party began to believe that universal benefits were becoming an anachronism in a society in which most people were relatively prosperous, compared to the 1930s and 40s. They argued that better uses could be found for 'middle class subsidies'.

However, it appeared that many Scottish voters held to the old social democratic virtues of progressive universalism and believed that education – higher as well as secondary – should be based on the ability to learn, not the ability to earn. There were also fears that erupted during the referendum campaign that the Scottish NHS was in danger from market reforms in the UK, begun by Labour after 2005, despite health being a devolved responsibility to Holyrood.[73] The introduction of £9,000 per year tuition fees in England by the Coalition government in December 2010 seemed to confirm Scots, not only in their rejection of tuition fees, but also in their hostility to the political culture of Westminster politics as a whole.

There was a growing belief in Scotland that market values had come to dominate both the main parties in Westminster and that Scotland was being taken down a neoliberal road begun by the hated Margaret Thatcher in the 1980s. And not only by Labour but also by the Liberal Democrats, who had a significant following in Scotland until 2010. The Scottish Liberal Democrats had signed a solemn and binding election 'pledge' never to introduce tuition fees, and suffered huge collateral damage from their leader Nick Clegg's U-turn and decision to form a coalition with the Conservatives after the 2010 General Election. In 2011, the Scottish Liberal Democrats – who had been in government with Labour since 1999 – crashed to disaster and lost most of their Holyrood MSPs. It was a foretaste of what was to come.

BETTER TOGETHER

Matters finally came to a head for Labour during the independence referendum in 2014. The Yes Scotland campaign pitched independence very much as a continuation of social democratic politics under another name. The Scottish Government's 670 page White Paper on independence, *Scotland's Future*, published in November 2013, read in many respects like a Labour manifesto from the 1970s or 80s – intentionally so. Its headline promise – free childcare – wasn't even strictly speaking an independence issue, since the Scottish Parliament already had power over childcare. However, the then Deputy First Minister, Nicola Sturgeon, who had largely drafted the document, insisted that only with independence would any Scottish administration be able to raise enough tax revenue to pay the £700m cost of the childcare policy.

The White Paper didn't explicitly call for higher taxation in Scotland but it certainly indicated a return to tax and spend, and to policies on open immigration, unilateral nuclear disarmament, and land reform, that were unmistakably left-wing. Its attitude to debt, borrowing and currency – and the problems of managing the transition to an independent Scotland – was very much from the Syriza school of national populist politics.

The dominant issue in the referendum campaign, however, was not social policy but the pound – specifically the decision by the Unionist parties of the cross-party Better Together campaign to refuse to contemplate allowing an independent Scotland to continue to use the pound as its national currency. Labour's leader Ed Miliband even promised to put a statement in Labour's manifesto that an independent Scotland would never under any circumstances be allowed to use the pound.[74] In *Disunited Kingdom*, my account of the referendum campaign and its immediate aftermath, I explore the extent to which this undermined for many Scots the moral foundation of the UK as a partnership of free nations in a voluntary union.

But the more immediate problem for the Labour Party was guilt by association with the Conservatives. The Better Together campaign was defined very much by elite interests: big businesses like Aggreko and BP, financial institutions like RBS and Standard Life, and, of course, the author of the 'Declaration on the Pound' of 13th February 2014, the combative Conservative Chancellor George Osborne. He is not the most popular politician in Scotland. By allying with the Tories and enthusiastically endorsing the Chancellor's diktat on currency, Labour handed the social democratic agenda largely to the SNP and the Yes groups.

This alliance with conservative interests did its greatest damage in Labour's heartland areas like Dundee, North Lanarkshire, and its citadel Glasgow. These working class constituencies turned in unprecedented numbers to the cause of independence in the final fatal weeks of the 2014 referendum campaign. Radicalised by groups like the Radical Independence Campaign with its mass canvasses, inspired by the left rhetoric of Alex Salmond, and attracted by the SNP's new leader and MSP for Glasgow Govan, Nicola Sturgeon, many long-standing Labour voters turned apparently overnight into SNP supporters. Opinion polls in the wake of the referendum suggested that the SNP would win a landslide, not only in future Holyrood elections, but also in future general elections.

No one really believed these opinion polls showing the nationalists with an unprecedented 20% lead over Labour. It was widely assumed after September 2014 that the referendum effect would be short lived and that Scottish politics would soon return to normal. It didn't. The shock of Johann Lamont's resignation, and the failure of the Better Together campaign to follow up its victory in the referendum, left the SNP with the political momentum. Then came Jim Murphy.

NEW JIM

The Scottish Labour leadership election in November 2014 was well-organised and fair. Jim Murphy faced the left-wing trade unionist and education spokesman Neil Findlay MSP, and a representative of the feminist-environmental strand of Labour politics in the shape of the former Scottish minister Sarah Boyack MSP. Of the three, Jim Murphy seemed by far the ablest candidate. One of the most energetic and forceful politicians in the party, Murphy had burst on the political scene in 1997 when he won the formerly safe Tory seat of Eastwood. By the time its name was changed to East Renfrewshire in 2005, he had turned it into a safe Labour seat.

Murphy had in many ways an ideal Labour back-story, which was one of the reasons the Scottish press were so fond of him. He grew up in struggling working class poverty in a Glasgow tenement where, it was claimed, he had had to sleep in a drawer because of lack of living space. His parents emigrated to South Africa in search of work, where young Jim saw the iniquities of apartheid and became a socialist. He is also a teetotaller, a vegetarian, and an authority on Scottish football – which he rarely lets anyone forget.

He returned to Scotland, became a student radical, and rose to President of the National Union of Students. The NUS has long been a royal road to the Labour Party parliamentary benches and Jim became a candidate after spending nine years as an NUS student activist (failing, as his detractors never fail to remind him, to graduate). In 1996, Murphy was given a crack at the 'unwinnable' seat of Eastwood. After he won it at the next year's UK general election, Murphy rose rapidly through the junior ministerial ranks and became Scottish Secretary under Gordon Brown in 2008.

Murphy did not thrive under Brown's successor Ed Miliband however. He was frozen out of the inner cabinet, and given the post of Overseas Development Secretary. But he saw a chance in the referendum of rebooting his career in Scotland, perhaps emulating Boris Johnson's success and prominence as London Mayor. During the referendum campaign Murphy made a pretty transparent leadership play by mounting a 100-town speaking tour of Scotland on an Irn Bru crate. He was not well received however, and he cut his tour short after being struck by an egg thrown by a nationalist demonstrator.

When he was elected as Scottish leader in December, he was given a positive welcome by the Scottish press who had become fed up with lacklustre Labour leaders and welcomed the opportunity to say something positive about the party for a change. Murphy is very much a media politician and has always judged his performance in terms of column inches, and also, allegedly, by the size of his press photographs. He immediately announced a raft of changes which he said would put the Scottish party on a new constitutional footing and give it a new radical edge. If the SNP had stolen Labour's social democratic clothes, he thought, why could Labour not steal them right back?

The problem here was that Jim Murphy came from the Blairite right-wing of the Labour party whose policies had been so comprehensively rejected by Scottish voters. He had been an enthusiastic and unapologetic supporter of nuclear weapons and he continued to be so. He refused to apologise for the war in Iraq. Murphy had supported the market reforms in the NHS in England and had voted for the restoration of tuition fees. He was also on record as being opposed to further tax-raising powers for the Scottish Parliament on the grounds that this would undermine the union.[75] How could Murphy carry off this political sex change convincingly?

New Jim began by reversing his opposition to free higher education and declared himself in favour of free prescription charges and bus passes for the elderly. He slapped down his education spokesman, Iain Gray, when he said that free school meals 'only benefitted the middle classes'.[76] He said that he was in favour of 'universalism' and of progressive taxation, and he staked his claim on the left by calling for the 50p tax band to be restored in Scotland even if it wasn't restored in England. The SNP had equivocated over this, and Alex Salmond seemed opposed to having a Scottish top rate in case it led to the departure of business.

On devolution Jim Murphy started claiming that he wanted maximum devolution, 'devo max', though this meant something different than full fiscal autonomy. He called for the devolution of welfare and the work programme to Holyrood.[77] He proposed a changed constitutional position for the Labour party, a 'New Clause 4' which would mean 'total devolution of policy formation' for the Scottish Party.[78] To cap it all, he declared that he 'wasn't a unionist' and that he wanted to appeal to 180,000 Yes voters to support Labour.[79]

Murphy's left neo-nationalism was rather contradicted by his 'dream team' of back-room staff. This included, as Chief of Staff, John McTernan, a long time Blair policy adviser and combative supporter of nuclear defence and market reforms in the NHS. Head of Strategy was Blair McDougall, the chair of Better Together, assisted by one of the most hostile anti-nationalist bloggers, Susan Dalgety. These were hardly the figures you would want around you if you were trying to be, as one insider put it, 'more Nat than the Nats'.

The new team set about trying to bamboozle Scottish voters with a flurry of populist proposals like ending the alcohol ban at football grounds and repealing the Offensive Behaviour At Football Grounds Act. Murphy said he was more opposed to fracking, or unconventional gas and shale drilling, than the SNP. He even pledged to re-nationalise rail. But the voters were not convinced. I wrote that Murphy was a little like a very good female impersonator – who wore the right clothes, could talk the talk and walked the walk – but then you noticed the telltale stubble on the chin. The Scottish voters were too sophisticated to fall for confusion marketing techniques and Murphy's popularity – never high – sank dramatically in the months before the General Election.

In the final weeks, Murphy abandoned the attempt to woo Yes voters and returned to a revised form of what was called 'Project Fear' during the independence referendum. He argued that the SNP's plans for fiscal autonomy would, like independence, be financially disastrous, leaving a £7.6bn 'black hole' in the accounts. It was, he said, 'Austerity Max'.[80] He unveiled a billboard with a bomb and the words 'SNP Full Fiscal Austerity Bombshell'. Some Labour activists started appealing to Tory and Liberal Democrat voters to tactically vote against the SNP, as was being urged by the right-wing *Scottish Daily Mail*.[81]

Turning attention to fiscal autonomy and revisiting the unionist alliance was probably the worst move Murphy's team could have made at this stage. The 45% who had voted for independence never accepted this account in the first place, and even many who had voted No in the independence referendum were left unmoved by Project Fear Two. Fiscal Autonomy was something they suspected would never happen, because the UK parties were opposed to it and Westminster would have to give its assent before Scotland acquired the full range of tax raising powers. All this did was undermine the attempt to demonstrate that Labour had changed, and reminded voters of the association with the Tories.

THE WORST TV LEADERS' DEBATE EVER

On television debates, the Labour leader joined with the Conservatives' Ruth Davidson and the LibDem leader, Willie Rennie, in barracking Nicola Sturgeon as if Better Together were still in existence. Murphy claimed that the SNP intended to impose another independence referendum as well as Full Fiscal Autonomy, a claim Sturgeon denied. The nadir was the BBC Scotland Sunday Politics debate on 12th April, styled the 'stair heir rammy' in the press, in which Murphy and the other unionist party leaders talked over an exasperated Nicola Sturgeon to such an extent that the entire discussion became unintelligible.[82] Except, that is, for one unfortunate comment from the Labour leader who said audibly that there would be 'no need for further cuts after 2016'. This was not Labour party policy. The next day the Shadow Chancellor himself Ed Balls hung Murphy out to dry by commenting: 'there will be cuts in non-protected areas.'[83] Labour's business spokesman Chuka Umunna added: 'The leader of the Scottish Labour Party will not be in charge of the UK budget.'[81] From there, there was no recovery. Wile E Coyote had finally run out of road.

UK Labour was clearly not in any mood to help Jim Murphy. It had its own problems with the Tories spreading a scare about the 'nightmare on Downing St', if Ed Miliband entered Number Ten with the support of the SNP. Such a government, said David Cameron, would not be 'legitimate'. This was nonsense of course, because any government is legitimate if and when it commands a majority of votes in the House of Commons. Indeed, the first ever Labour government in 1924 was just such a minority. However, rather than contradicting Cameron's misleading account of the British constitutional practice, Ed Miliband seemed to endorse it. On BBC's Question Time Special on 29th April, the Labour leader announced that he would 'rather not govern' in the UK if it meant 'doing a deal' with the SNP.

This offended even many non-nationalists in Scotland. Mr Miliband appeared to be saying that it was legitimate to 'do deals' with the Liberal Democrats, the Social Democratic and Labour Party, or even the Northern Irish Democratic Unionist Party, but not with the duly elected representatives of Scotland.

In any situation where no party has an overall majority it is the duty of all the parties to seek arrangements that could form a stable government. That is an essential requirement of any parliamentary democracy. It appeared to many that Ed Miliband was endorsing the Tory claim that Scottish MPs did not have legitimacy in the House of Commons if they voted against a Conservative Queen's Speech.

This couldn't have been more damaging to the Scottish Labour Party in a UK election marred by shocking anti-Scottish rhetoric from Tory MPs like Owen Paterson who said that 'the Scots' were using English tax payers as 'a piggy bank'.[84] Meanwhile, Nicola Sturgeon was becoming a huge success in the UK debates. It was turning into Labour MPs' worst nightmare. Some simply gave up. The Glasgow MP Tom Harris took to posting vines of himself dragging his dog across a carpet saying that he was 'bored with politics'.[85] Whole swathes of Scotland's Labour campaigning virtually stopped as the party focused its resources on defending the seats of big names in the party like Shadow Scottish Secretary Margaret Curran in Glasgow East, to the dismay of party workers in lesser constituencies.[86]

The election night itself was heartbreaking for Labour as safe seat after safe seat fell to the hated SNP. A clean sweep in Glasgow; all of Tayside; nearly all of Edinburgh. Scottish politics is tribal, and the enmity between Labour and SNP is intense despite many of their policies and much of their social philosophies being broadly similar. The atmosphere at the counts in the big cities was tense and acrimonious – though peaceful. The nadir came at 4.00am on BBC Scotland's Election 2015 programme when Ian Davidson – who had famously said during the referendum campaign that all that remained for the victorious unionists was to 'bayonet the wounded' – stuck the bayonet in Murphy's back. 'He should do the honourable thing and resign,' he said.

But Murphy, unlike Alex Salmond, didn't do the decent

thing. He clung on for over a month during which he sparked a near civil war in the movement by accusing the Unite leader Len McCluskey of being the architect of Scottish Labour's misfortune.[87] It was an awkward exit and infuriated those in the party who were hoping for some measure of reconciliation after defeat. But Murphy's parting shots did at least force Labour to address fundamental questions about its constitution. Was it acceptable in the age of one member one vote for the Scottish leader still to be elected by an electoral college in which one third of votes were assigned to the trades unions? Could Labour in Scotland continue in business dealing with the left-wing rhetoric of the SNP while the UK Labour Party appeared to be going in the opposite ideological direction?

Labour in Scotland is now in a very dark place, as the gloomy Labour MP John Cruddas might have put it. Kezia Dugdale could undoubtedly make a worthy leader, but at thirty-four she is inexperienced. She only entered parliament in 2011. She is also, ironically, a member of Len McCluskey's Unite. Labour clearly cannot continue in its present form and she has a huge task making the decisive break from the past that is needed if the party is to regain the trust and support of Scottish voters. It may be that only with a name change and a new constitutional relationship to the UK party will Scottish Labour be able to remain in contention in Scotland.

PASOKIFCATION

With the SNP dominating not just the centre ground but also the centre left, it is a moot point whether there remains any space left for Labour. Murphy tried to outflank the SNP on the left and it didn't work. Arguably, the space in Scottish politics right now lies on the right of the SNP, where there must be a natural small 'c' conservative and unionist vote. But 'Tory' is still a four letter word in Scotland and it simply isn't an option for Labour to pitch its tent on the right of the SNP. Anyway, it is occupied by the able Ruth Davidson, the youthful leader of the Scottish Tories.

There is no natural right for any political party to continue in business in today's shifting political environment. The Scottish Unionist Party dominated Scottish politics in the 1950s until it formally changed its name to the Conservatives and Unionists. By 1997 it had been wiped out in Scotland and the Conservatives have never recovered. 2015 was their worst share of the vote in 100 years. There is a danger that Labour's defeat in Scotland may also have been so severe as to lead to what is called 'Pasokification' – after the fate of the Greek socialist party Pasok, which was destroyed as an electoral force by the left-wing Syriza coalition in Greece. Labour figures like the former Scottish Minister Andy Kerr, and the former leadership contender Neil Findlay, argued that only by asserting its constitutional autonomy from UK Labour, and adopting a radical home rule agenda, could Labour get into contention with the SNP. If it did not, said Kerr, Labour would 'die like the dinosaurs'.[88]

Ironically, it was Len McCluskey's favourite UK Labour leadership candidate Andy Burnham who suggested on the BBC's Andrew Marr Show on 16th May 2015 there was 'a case' for a separate Scottish Labour Party.[89] Neil Kinnock's son Stephen suggested that the Scottish Labour Party should be renamed the SDLP, the 'Scottish Democratic Labour Party'.[90] A name change is a good idea, but this might sound too like the Social Democratic and Labour Party that stands in Northern Ireland. Labour wouldn't want to be connected, even in terms of nomenclature, with the politics of the province.

Really the only serious contender must be the Independent Labour Party. There's a strong sense of Scottish tradition here because this was the party of Maxton, Wheatley, and Manny Shinwell. Originally pacifist, the Independent Labour Party effectively split from the official Labour Party in 1931 over the austerity regime of the National Government of Ramsay MacDonald (who ironically had been an Independent Labour Party member himself). The ILP faded after the war but it is remembered with some affection in left-wing circles. The main objection of such a name change might be that it would sound too much like the SNP because of the word 'independence'. But, of course, the old Independent Labour Party had nothing to do with Scottish independence, which simply wasn't an issue in those days. It was about ideological independence.

The ILP was a party with profound Scottish, pacifist, socialist, and anti-imperialist principles. If the Labour Party in Scotland is serious about change, it has to make a serious change. It seems to me that becoming the Independent Labour Party and having a one member one vote structure is the only way Labour can get back into the game. It must avoid making the same mistake as the Scottish Tories after their wipe out in 1997: sticking with a toxic brand name. One legacy – perhaps unintended – of the Murphy leadership is that he laid the ground for a possible breakaway. His new 'Clause 4' of the party constitution, asserting that the Scottish party was its own boss and had 'total devolution of policy making', may have been regarded as a gimmick. But it is still there. As is his support for those universalist left-wing policies like the rejection of tuition fees. It would be the supreme irony of Labour politics if Jim Murphy, the Blairite unionist, should have been the midwife of a new neo-nationalist Independent Labour Party.

However, it seems unlikely that the Scottish Labour Party will make a break from the UK party. Kezia Dugdale has come out against it, as has the UK leadership. She said on BBC TV on June 7th that: 'I favour a much more autonomous Scottish Labour Party, I'd like to see us set our own policy here but I don't support an independent party, I think that's wrong.' Of Labour's UK leadership contenders, all but the left-wing Jeremy Corbyn, rejected the idea of a separate Scottish Labour

Party. Yvette Cooper said it was important to retain the current relationship with UK Labour because of the party's 'shared values'. However, given the rightward drift of the UK party towards 'aspirational' pro-business policies, this suggests that Labour in Scotland will continue largely on its present course. This means that there is now a real possibility the remaining territory on the left of the SNP may soon be occupied by one of the new political formations spawned by the referendum experience. As will be explained in the next chapter, the Radical Independence Campaign emerged as the strongest element of the non-aligned Yes campaign and intends to form a new Scottish party of the left. But any new Syriza-style party of the Left clearly would have to avoid some of the personality and ideological divisions that have riven the Scottish Left in the past, and have started to emerge in the non-aligned independence movement. It is to these divisions that we must now turn.

Chapter Five:

The Yes Disalliance

On Saturday 24th April 2015, a couple of thousand people turned up in Glasgow's George Square under the banner 'Hope over Fear' to recreate the raucous flag-waving, face-painting spirit of the Glasgow referendum campaign. Nationalist bikers roared around the square on their Harleys. The troubadour Gerry Cinnamon sang his anthem of the same name. 'Hope over fear... don't be afraid... tell Westminster Tories Scotland's no longer your slave'.

It wasn't an SNP rally and Nicola Sturgeon stayed well away, even though the stage was decked with the slogan 'Lend your votes to the SNP'. Its figurehead, the former Scottish Socialist MSP and anti-poll tax campaigner Tommy Sheridan, urged the throng to send a message to Westminster by voting out the 'Red Tories' of the Scottish Labour Party. The largely working class audience, dressed in kilts and T-shirts saying unprintable things about Conservative politicians, cheered and chanted as if their team has just won the cup.

Robin McAlpine, the influential leader of the pro-independence think tank and news service The Common Weal, gave one of his usual rapid fire speeches, sounding like an evangelist on speed. He was full of enthusiasm for the 'people's revolution' that was sweeping Scotland and creating new possibilities for social change. He avoided direct references to the Hope over Fear organisers, and pledged only conditional support for the SNP. However, no sooner had he stood down than the non-aligned independence movement was rocked by one of the most acrimonious disputes it has experienced in its short life.

McAlpine was condemned by women's groups, the Scottish Socialist Party, Radical Independence Campaign activists, and members of his own Common Weal group, for attending the Hope over Fear rally and sharing a platform with Tommy Sheridan. The former leader of the SSP has become persona non grata on the Scottish Left. Scott MacDonald, speaking on behalf of the Edinburgh North and Leith Common Weal group, blogged that McAlpine had delivered an 'incredible insult' to Women for Independence and 'true socialists' by speaking alongside 'the convicted perjurer, misogynist and abuser' Tommy Sheridan.

This is a reference to Tommy Sheridan's infamous conviction for lying during his defamation case against the *News of the World* in 2006. The tabloid had made allegations about the former Scottish Socialist Party leader's fondness for attending swingers bars. He had won the initial defamation action and received £200,000 in damages. But in a controversial move, the Crown Office later successfully prosecuted Sheridan for perjury after members of the SSP provided evidence that he had not been telling the truth.

The affair split the Scottish Socialist Party from top to bottom and led to it losing all of its six MSPs in the Holyrood parliamentary elections in 2007. The case also made Sheridan a hate figure among women's groups. This was because of his personal morality and because of suggestions that he 'abused' women in the SSP by pressuring them to lie under oath. 'Sheridan vilified the women in the party who refused to bow to him,' said the former SSP MSP Rosie Kane. 'Our lives have been devastated by his actions.'[91]

Sheridan denies these allegations against him. He says that he has been the victim of a cabal of women in the Scottish Socialist Party who wanted to turn it 'from a class-based party to a gender-obsessed one'.[92] Sheridan also felt partially vindicated by the collapse of the *News of the World* following the phone hacking scandal. Sheridan's accuser, the former

Editor of the *News of the World* Andy Coulson, found himself in the High Court in Edinburgh accused of perjury in May 2015. But though Coulson had been imprisoned for phone hacking, he was exonerated by the Scottish judge on the grounds that his alleged lies about the practice were not relevant to the Sheridan perjury case.[93]

Robin McAlpine wrote a spirited defence of his decision to share a platform with Tommy Sheridan on the pro-independence website Bella Caledonia.[94] He said that he opposed 'blacklists' on principle because they 'took away people's judgement' and 'suppress debate'. He went on to talk favourably about the organisers of Hope over Fear and suggested that its critics were too middle class: 'Like it or not, Hope over [Fear] is the only truly working class part of our wider campaign.' He said that the broader independence movement could not afford to reject the 'bawdy and raucous' Hope over Fear, which had organised a series of mass rallies during the referendum campaign. 'I am greatly worried that the predominantly middle class part of the movement has a tendency to assume that there is something lesser about Hope Over Fear.'

McAlpine concluded with an appeal to the independence movement to avoid the original sin of the Left: factionalism. 'Imagine if Women for Indy could have joined the carnival. Imagine if Radical Independence Campaign could have been there in strength. Imagine if we could have been hugging each other rather than tweeting about each other... No movement is immortal. No movement can survive division after division... Please let us find a way to balance our ethical and moral purity with tolerance, accommodation and solidarity.'

His appeal fell on deaf ears, however, and the comment pages of Bella Caledonia fizzed with indignation. 'It seems Robin McAlpine is fine about throwing women under a bus to protect and enhance the standing of a liar, criminal and an abusive man,' said one of many irate posters. 'A space containing

Citizen Tommy is not a safe space for women,' said another. 'Terrible excuses made by McAlpine. He clearly doesn't care about Sheridan's victims. Mealy, mouthed disgrace.' Members of the press joined in too. *The Herald*'s political correspondent Tom Gordon tweeted: 'Robin McAlpine now using Common Space to defend backing Tommy Sheridan's astro-trot front group.' The suggestion here, presumably, was that Sheridan's political party, Solidarity, was behind the Hope over Fear rallies, and that they were not spontaneous expressions of working class support for independence. Mind you, the forthcoming general election was to prove that there is no shortage of spontaneous support for the SNP in Glasgow.

However, some commentators defended Robin McAlpine's objection to blacklists. 'Without the working class, the middle class art school clique which is a wonderful, creative part of this movement, will, in short order, find themselves only talking amongst themselves.' One bewildered Yes supporter described the entire row as a Monty Python 'People's Front of Judea scenario'. It was indeed sounding horribly reminiscent of the divisions that always seem to afflict the far left in the twentieth century, albeit combined with the twenty-first century notion that 'the personal is political' and that sexual morality is as important as ideology.

NATIONAL COLLECTIVE VERSUS LOKI THE RAPPER

It seemed that a class divide had begun to emerge in what had loosely been called the continuing 'Yes Alliance', the various non-SNP groups that had campaigned for independence in the referendum. The reference to an 'art school clique' related to criticism that National Collective, the acclaimed arts-based indyref initiative, tended to exclude working class people. Co-founded by the graphic designer Ross Colquhoun in 2012, the Collective had mobilised some 4,000 writers, artists, poets, and designers, and organised a series of festivals, or Yestivals, of music, poetry and comedy which lent much-needed colour and energy to the Yes campaign. However, some in the wider independence movement felt that its art was rather conservative, inward-looking, and middle class. As McAlpine himself put it: '[working class supporters of Hope over Fear] don't really do wish trees and coffee mornings and performance poetry and deliberative conferences.'

The rapper Loki, real name Darren McGarvey, inspired a vivid debate on the Nationalist left when he posted a series of video blogs in March 2015 saying that he and working class artists felt excluded from National Collective.[95] In one memorable rant worthy of Malcolm Tucker, he said that National Collective existed only to 'suck Ross Colquhoun's rugby cock'. He later apologised for that remark. For their part, National Collective insisted that there had been no attempt to exclude anybody from the organisation. In fact, they say that they discussed a funding project with him to engage young working class people. The whole point of National Collective was that anyone could participate and there was no attempt to curate any of the material it published or staged.

More seriously, however, Loki also criticised National Collective for being too close to government after it emerged in March 2015 that Ross Colquhoun had joined the SNP payroll as an 'engagement strategist'. 'His appointment by Scotland's ruling party,' said Loki, 'is sure to raise questions regarding National Collective's authenticity as the artistic voice of the Yes movement.' Loki was joined in the assault on National Collective's integrity by the Yes-supporting journalist Andrew Eaton Lewis, the former Arts Editor of the *Scotsman*. While he paid tribute to its member's creative work and energy, he criticised the Collective for lacking any kind of internal accountability, membership rights, or constitution. It had, he said, a 'democratic deficit'.

The truth is National Collective was never a democracy. It was an association of like-minded individuals who came together in an ad hoc way to try to inject some colour into the Yes Scotland campaign, which was, by common agreement, too preoccupied with dry statistics and abstract arguments about currency. Initially the Collective was arguably more like a writing group than a political or arts organisation. But the initiative simply struck the right note at the right time, gathered hundreds of volunteers, and unleashed a huge amount of anarchic creative energy. True, it wasn't Turner Prize stuff, but they weren't interested in selling to the arts market or being placed in galleries.

National Collective's relationship to the SNP was always close since a number of founder members were SNP supporters, but it kept the other organisations, including Yes Scotland, very much at arms length. It is unfair on the artists, musicians, comedians, writers, fashion designers, and others who gave their time for free to the Yestivals and other events to complain that it was a nationalist front. It wasn't. Political parties simply aren't capable of having that much fun for a start. There was perhaps an element of naïveté in believing that the Collective could continue as a free-form, come-as-you-are 'happening' when it started raising significant sums of money and had become a national movement. But it never pretended to be a political party. As Christopher Silver, one of National Collective's prominent members put it on Twitter: 'The lesson I took from indyref is that it's better to start your own revolution than wait around for one with an AGM.'

The debate raging in Bella Caledonia soon attracted the attention of political journalists from the mainstream press. Many had never rated National Collective and had been waiting for an opportunity to have a go at it: 'I don't care whether National Collective are democrats,' wrote the Spectator columnist Alex Massie in the *Scotsman*, 'I'd just prefer them to be artists.'[96] He quoted sections of bad poetry that had been published on the website. He might equally have quoted the celebrated Scottish poet Liz Lochhead or the Booker prize-winning novelist James Kelman who contributed to the hardback almanac *Inspired by Independence.* Or one of Scotland's leading playwrights, David Greig, who said that National Collective had brought inspiration to the independence debate.

But, for my money, the success of National Collective had nothing to do with the arts-world names that it attracted. Any campaign can do that. It wasn't trying to appeal to the arts establishment or bid for Arts Council grants. What was endearing and new about National Collective was the involvement of unimportant people who were invited to contribute their poetry, thoughts, art, photography, humour, knitting, or whatever, without being subjected to withering criticism. National Collective set itself the task of 'imagining a better Scotland', and even the much-derided wish trees did exactly that.

Unfortunately the scorn, accusations of class bias, and political selling out seemed to undermine the confidence of those still involved in the Collective in late 2014/15. It was always on shifting sands based on voluntary effort and changing personnel. Despite its communication skills it seemed to lack the will to mount an effective defence of its work in political or artistic terms, even though its success was never in doubt. It is one of those occasions when some old media PR might have helped. Perhaps even a press conference to address some of the political accusations formally. But it didn't happen, and within a month, National Collective effectively shut up shop.

The criticism that it was a clique of middle class luvvies was probably the killing blow. Middle class radicals in Scotland tend to be insecure of their class background. There is no obvious reason for this sensitivity since revolutionaries from Karl Marx to Nelson Mandela have invariably emerged from the middle classes. It's what you say that matters, not where you come from. But in Scotland there is a degree of class hostility that can be very difficult to manage if you are on the sharp end of it. The dark side of Scotland's literary strand of proletarian romanticism is a cultural animosity toward people who didn't grow up on housing estates. Or who don't sound as if they do. The final irony of the National Collective class row is that Ross Colquhoun was brought up in a single parent household in Edinburgh's Drylaw estate.

On May 1st 2015, a statement on National Collective laid the movement to rest. 'To be part of it was exciting, energising, inspiring and beautiful. National Collective belongs to a time and a place and that moment has passed.' If the implication here was that National Collective had always been time-limited, that wasn't entirely true. It had never been the Collective's intention to liquidate itself after the referendum and initially it had ambitious plans to become a permanent, non-aligned, arts-based organisation. Aware that it had been too urban and lowland-centred, the organisers had planned to develop its network of local groups across Scotland and publish a series of arts-based journals in each of these areas. It sent out questionnaires to its 4,000 odd members and was seeking crowdfunding for this purpose. But, as the controversy surrounding the organisation mounted, these ideas faded. The energy had drained out of the Collective and an organisation that had been built on nothing had to eventually recognise that it had no visible means of support. It is worth however considering its last will and testament:

National Collective offered a form of participation in politics that was thoroughly imaginative, but also accessible to all. National Collective tapped into the consciousness of a generation for whom the restrictions of ideological and party loyalties can often seem stifling and archaic. National Collective's central aim, to 'imagine a better Scotland', remains just as relevant now that the referendum campaign is over. Its early success was just one example of a wider upsurge in grassroots activity in support of Scottish independence. However the group was also tapping another seam, namely, the rise of what has been described as the 'precariat'. The young, often highly educated post-industrial workforce that has become an ever more significant feature of neoliberal economies everywhere. National Collective is what a political campaign looks like when it is instigated and sustained by such people.

That was a remarkable statement in many ways, both in its maturity and its political wisdom. It was fully aware of its limitations but also confident about its strengths. Of course, it was unreasonable to expect young people with careers to build to give endlessly of their time for nothing. It probably couldn't have continued without proper funding and some kind of permanent secretariat. And there is much good work continuing by people involved in the venture. Nevertheless, when National Collective was extinguished, a light went out in the independence movement. I wasn't involved in National Collective in any way and hope someone who was closer than I was to National Collective writes a proper assessment of its achievements. If Scotland is in the middle of a democratic revolution, then National Collective deserves a lot more than a footnote.

TRANSPHOBIA, MISOGYNY, HOMOPHOBIA, AND WHATEVER

The demise of National Collective seemed to epitomise the failure of the continuing Yes movement or alliance to find a collective way forward in the post-referendum era. In place of the infectious enthusiasm and optimism of the referendum, there was now an element of division, rancor, and disillusion. Perhaps this is just what always happens to radical movements. Yet it was a strange moment for cultural defeatism. The day National Collective folded the opinion polls were indicating that the SNP was on course to win every seat in Scotland. That, you might think, was an eloquent rebuff to Alex Massie who had said that National Collective's radicalism was about 'as subversive as a flat white in Finnieston'.[97] Finnieston is in Glasgow which was the prime focus of the nationalist electoral revolution on May 7th 2015. History may judge that the 'hipster unco guid' as he called them, played a not insignificant role in turning the young people of that city to the SNP.

One reason the SNP came roaring out of the referendum defeat in September 2014 was precisely the existence of the wider nationalist movement that had been created during the referendum campaign. Organisations like Common Weal, Hope over Fear, National Collective, Women for Independence, and the Radical Independence Campaign had provided portals through which thousands of ordinary voters could be introduced to civic nationalism without feeling that they were being sold a party line. In an age when politicians of all parties are held in the greatest suspicion this was a huge benefit to the independence campaign. But class and gender tensions were really beginning to damage the non-aligned movement in 2015. Wings Over Scotland, run by former Liberal Democrat and ordained minister Stuart Campbell, was the next target for sustained criticism.

Wings Over Scotland is an extraordinarily successful one-man, pro-independence website run by Rev. Stuart Campbell from Bath, Somerset. 'Rev. Stu' played a major role in proselytising the case for independence during the referendum with a freely distributed 'Wee Blue Book' of arguments for voting Yes which had a print run of over 250,000. During 2014, the referendum year, Wings blogs were read by 2.9m unique readers (53.6m page views), verified by Google analytics. That is an extraordinary reach. Campbell provided a running commentary on the excesses of the unionist press throughout the campaign and after it. The press hate Wings Over Scotland, not least because it is a rival. But for hundreds of thousands of Scots it was an invaluable source of facts and arguments with which to challenge the predominantly unionist messages of the mainstream media. In 2014 alone, Campbell raised over £100,000 in six weeks in his annual crowdfunding appeal. Any understanding of Scotland's electoral revolution has to begin with social media, and Wings Over Scotland is arguably the dominant force on the indyref Internet.

Campbell has had repeated run-ins with the Labour-supporting mass circulation tabloid, the *Daily Record*. In February 2015, after reporting it to the Independent Press Standards Organisation, IPSO, Wings secured a correction from the *Daily Record* over its coverage of the Smith Commission proposals for having 'significantly misrepresented the fiscal consequences of the Smith Commission's recommendations'. The *Record* responded with an editorial condemning Wings Over Scotland as 'a world of conspiracy theories, hatred and paranoia'.[98]

At its best Wings Over Scotland is intelligent, boisterous, informed and progressive. Unfortunately, the Rev. Stu has a penchant for using harsh language, and he is inclined to refer to his critics as 'wankstains' and other offensive appellations. For this reason it has been so easy for the press to cast him as a foul-mouthed 'cybernat' who should not be taken seriously. However, while he takes no prisoners in arguments on Twitter, I have never in all the years I have followed him known Campbell to be overtly homophobic or sexist. Yet he has acquired a reputation for being both. Indeed, many in the pro-independence women's movement seem to believe that he is an outright misogynist and Campbell has also been accused of 'transmisogyny'.[99] The allegations feature in posts from the Burdz Eye View blogger Kate Higgins, who is now a special adviser to the First Minister, and in independence-supporting blogs such as Better Nation.[100]

Campbell's alleged offences appear to have begun with remarks he made to a female victim of sexual abuse in 2008. He objected to a post from American feminist Cara Kulwicki who claimed a comedy routine by Johnny Vegas justified rape. Stuart Campbell took issue with her definition of rape. He allegedly posted on a US message board to the effect that there is a difference between penetration with a finger and full scale intercourse. Kulwicki has since taken down the relevant pages from the Internet so it is difficult to judge this. But Campbell insists he did not try to justify rape as such.

Campbell is also on record as once saying in 2012 that 'feminism is the most intolerant ideology currently operating in the UK',[101] and he made disrespectful remarks about men 'pretending' to be women during the Bradley/Chelsea Manning case.[102] But the main cause of Campbell's feminist blacklisting seems to be a piece he wrote on 4th March 2012 entitled 'Ugly Witches are Easy to Hunt' on the case of the former SNP MP Bill Walker.[103]

Walker had that day been suspended by the SNP over claims of domestic abuse for which he was subsequently prosecuted in August 2013. In the piece above, Campbell argued that the 'allegations' about Walker in that day's *Sunday Herald* were 'unproven', which at the time they undoubtedly were. I have read this very carefully many times and I don't think any reasonable person could see this article in itself as sexist or attempting to justify domestic violence, just that there was a rush to judgement. Indeed, in the same article, Campbell says Walker should resign anyway on account of his proven 'homophobia'.

Stuart Campbell can answer for himself on these episodes and he does so robustly. People are free to draw their own conclusions. He undoubtedly uses unacceptable language, but there is a difference between disputing a definition of rape and being in favour of rape. Similarly, his alleged remarks in a casual conversation about Chelsea Manning 'not having tits' may seem unpleasant and transphobic in the widest sense, but they are hardly grounds for banishment to outer darkness.

Like Tommy Sheridan, 'Rev. Stu' describes himself as working class and has suggested that the resentment against him is partly because of his class background and his robust argumentative style. I don't know if this is justified or not, but there does appear to be an eagerness to condemn. His sweary and often aggressive tweets are arguably abusive in the broadest sense. If that kind of language is inherently misogynist then perhaps by that definition he is. But even stringing all the offensive Rev. Stu quotes above together, I do not believe anyone could claim he is guilty of outright sexism, homophobia, or transphobia. He has argued against all-women shortlists, but if that is sexist then so are SNP MSPs like Christine Graham who spoke against this policy at the 2015 SNP conference.

Throughout 2015, the 'continuing' Yes movement appeared to be on a hair-trigger for signs of sexism, transphobia, and other offences against sexual identity. There seems to me to be a danger that the middle class intellectuals who have tended to set the tone of discussion about independence will alienate people who do not always express themselves in what might be called refined or politically correct speech. The Internet is not a university seminar. Nor is it a feminist consciousness-raising group. It is important to distinguish between people who are genuinely intolerant of sexual minorities and those who simply use infelicitous language when talking about them. The independence movement must also avoid the narcissism of small differences if it doesn't want to suffer the same fate as the far left in the twentieth century.

THE INDEPENDENCE OF
WOMEN FOR INDEPENDENCE

Shortly after the publication of my book *Disunited Kingdom* in December 2014, some members of Women for Independence said I had misrepresented the group by suggesting that it was merely a subdivision of the Yes Scotland campaign. I thought I had made clear in Chapter One that Women for Independence was 'a parallel organisation'. But I realise that later reference may have given the impression that Women for Independence had been an organisational part of the official Yes Scotland campaign. This was not what I meant and I'm happy to correct this here. Women for Independence was always financially, organisationally, and ideologically separate from the Yes Scotland campaign. It made an enormous contribution to the referendum campaign by demonstrating that nationalism was not the property of the old patriarchal politics, and that independence was not just about Alex Salmond and the Scottish National Party.

This very minor episode did, however, illustrate something else about the post referendum period. The various groupings involved in the non-aligned independence movement were often anxious about having their identity subsumed or effaced by other political organisations and parties. This coincided with an understandable concern that the SNP might simply absorb all the non-nationalist organisations that had fought for independence. There had already been a serious bust-up over SNP heavy handedness early on in the referendum campaign, which led to a walk out by the Green Party (though they later rejoined Yes Scotland).[104] Given the power and influence of the SNP, and the character of its leader, Alex Salmond, it was quite understandable that organisations like Women for Independence did not want to be absorbed. It is an unfortunate irony, then, that the Scottish National Party has in effect become the only game in town.

There had been moves after the referendum in late 2014, if not to merge the various strands of the campaign, at least to provide an overall structure outwith the SNP by creating a broadly-based Yes Alliance or home rule campaign. There was even a proposal – initially endorsed by the SNP – that the Yes campaign should continue as a 'Yes Alliance' and could field its own candidates in the 2015 General Election. The deputy leader of the SNP, Stuart Hosie, even suggested that the SNP might back Yes Alliance candidates.[105] What he said was this:

> I have no doubt that the SNP can and will send the largest ever number of SNP MPs to Westminster at next year's general election, but if we can build a Yes Alliance, there is an opportunity to do even more than that. What is also clear is that whether we campaign on a joint platform of maximum powers for Scotland, or select candidates from the range of hugely talented people who emerged through the referendum campaign, the SNP should show the same willingness to work with individuals and organisations to make sure the largest number of Independence supporting MPs is delivered to Westminster next year.

This was a remarkable concession in many ways, especially given the burgeoning membership of the SNP. It was suggested that individuals like the actor Elaine C. Smith or the journalist Lesley Riddoch might stand as Yes Alliance candidates, though neither gave any indication themselves that they planned to do so. In the end, there were no independent candidates willing to put themselves forward in the General Election in 2015, and the idea of a Yes Alliance as an electoral gambit died. However, the SNP did open their candidates list to new members though they had to agree to support the party whip.

If nothing else, this demonstrates how difficult it is for individuals to develop both the self-confidence and the support necessary to stand for election to parliament as independents outside a political party. Even SNP incomers were thin on the ground. Out of all the 56 MPs elected in the 2015 General Election all but two, the Stranraer businessman Richard Arkless and Tommy Sheppard, were long-time SNP members. The SNP drove all before it. Perhaps this was inevitable given the extraordinary growth of Scottish nationalism, but it did raise the serious problem of where non-nationalists and home rule supporters – still the vast majority of Scottish voters – were to go now.

POP-UP CONSTITUTIONAL CONVENTION

On the 25th October 2014, an ad hoc gathering of representatives of National Collective, Common Weal, Women for Independence, the Independence Convention, Radical Independence Campaign, and others came together in Glasgow. They called themselves, for want of a better phrase, The Way Forward. This group discussed the possibilities of building a political alliance that would be distinct from the Scottish National Party and would campaign broadly not for independence as such but for home rule. At the time it appeared obvious that independence had been rejected in the referendum by a significant margin but that there were very many Scottish voters who wanted devolution max or radical home rule and were not content with the status quo or what had been offered by the Unionist parties in the 'Vow'. There were also some fears that the success of Better Together might create a reaction against autonomy for the Scottish parliament, and might even lead to curbs on its existing powers. This may seem somewhat ludicrous now, but in the weeks after the defeat of the independence campaign, anything seemed possible.

There was serious discussion at the Way Forward meeting of the possibility that the Independence Convention – a broad non-party independence grouping based around the actor Elaine C. Smith – might change its name to the Home Rule Convention. The intention was to reignite some of the spirit of the Scottish Constitutional Convention of the 1980s which had brought together trade unions, political parties, churches, charities and some councils to campaign for the restoration of the Scottish parliament. Led by Canon Kenyan Wright, the Scottish Constitutional Convention famously drafted the Sovereignty Declaration that was signed by all but one of the Scottish Labour MPs – the dissenter being the author of the West Lothian Question, Tam Dalyell.

In an article in the *Sunday Herald* in October 2014, I had made a half-serious proposal about setting up a 'pop-up convention' to have direct representation of 'Scottish civil society' on the Smith Commission on further devolution which was just being set up.[106] My concern was that Smith was simply being put together as a four party stitch-up and that the wider non-SNP home rule movement was being excluded. Yet in the past it had been civil initiatives that had driven the movement for constitutional change, not professional politicians. If the Smith Commission, the realisation of Gordon Brown's so-called 'Vow' to create devolution max was to be legitimate, I thought it should at least have direct representation from non-parliamentary bodies like the Scottish Trades Union Congress, the Scottish Council for Voluntary Organisations, Radical Independence, Women for Independence etc.

However, this idea was unattractive to many in the putative Yes Alliance who felt, rightly, that the constitutional convention was really a structure from the past that was not relevant to the new political conjuncture in Scotland. A number of people at the Way Forward meeting felt that such a body would merely reproduce the elite politics and patriarchy of the 'great and the good'. The future needed to be 'grassroots-based', not sponsored by establishment figures like Henry McLeish, however well meaning. Some objected to the idea of churches being involved in any constitutional campaign. Any way you looked at it, a pop-up convention was clearly a non-starter and I accepted that. As Zen mystics say, you can't step in the same river twice.

However, it left unresolved the question of how the broader home rule movement should be constituted and how it too could prevent itself becoming the wholly owned property of the Scottish National Party. The problem was that the Yes Scotland campaign, led by the former BBC news chief Blair Jenkins, had simply closed down after the referendum and effectively handed its huge membership and its thousands of followers on social media over to the SNP. This wasn't some Stalinist takeover as has been suggested, though there was internal criticism of the way Alex Salmond had micromanaged the referendum campaign. The SNP didn't want to have another branch structure in parallel to its own, so the 200 or so local Yes groups were somewhat cut adrift. Many of the local Yes groups continued – I spoke to a number of them myself. However, post referendum there was now no focus for their energies. The absence of a formal continuing Yes Alliance created a vacuum in the non-aligned independence campaign.

The proposal of turning the Independence Convention into a Home Rule Convention in the new year did not bear fruit, though Elaine C. Smith is still very much in business.

A rather different Home Rule Campaign was then set up by the chairman of Reform Scotland, Ben Thompson, involving nationalists like the former MSP Andrew Wilson and non-nationalists like the former Liberal Democrat Margaret Smith. But this was essentially a vehicle to promote discussion of new fiscal arrangements for the Scottish parliament. It did not have any retentions beyond that.

SCOTDEMOS: A NEW DEPARTURE FOR THE NATIONALIST LEFT

I don't want to sound too pessimistic here. There is still tremendous energy in the independence movement outside the SNP. Common Weal is now established as arguably one of the most progressive think tanks (McAlpine always prefers the phrase 'do tank') in the UK. It is trying to put intellectual substance into the arguments against austerity economics and establish a Nordic-style alternative to global financial capitalism. Robin McAlpine believes rightly that one of the failings of the Yes Scotland campaign was its inability to argue convincingly for a Scottish currency. Common Space also shows great promise as an alternative news service to the mainstream media.

It would be most unfortunate if the controversy over Robin McAlpine's appearance on the stage with Tommy Sheridan, and other concerns about the hiring policies of Common Weal (in November 2014 it was criticised for advertising for unpaid barristas in its Edinburgh cafe) were to damage this work.[107] Unfortunately, factionalism and adverse publicity does discourage the donations upon which ventures like this depend. All the Yes supporting groups have, like National Collective, faced difficulties trying to make the transition from being ad hoc campaigns into legally-constituted and properly-funded organisations run by paid employees not volunteers.

Women for Independence continues to be one of the most vigorous and broadly based 'alternative' campaigns of the SNP. It still attracts up to 1000 women to its gatherings. It has great influence over the policy of the Scottish government through the new First Minister Nicola Sturgeon who is very much a part of WFI, as it is sometimes called. Indeed, since many of its leading figures have been elected to Westminster, including the co-founder of Women for Independence, Natalie McGarry, it is likely to have a considerable influence on UK political debate.

The Radical Independence Campaign, co-founded by Jonathan Shafi, which brought together left groups like the Scottish Socialist Party and the Greens, is still going strong. At its conference in the Glasgow Armadillo on 24th November 2014, representatives of federated left groups like Podemos in Spain and Syriza discussed how their experience could be relevant to Scotland. The campaign has also been arguing for another referendum on independence and fully intends to be an important part of any future campaign.

The Radical Independence Campaign played a significant role during the referendum in mobilising working class communities in deprived areas like Glasgow's Easterhouse. This has helped radicalise a new generation of young activists like nineteen-year-old Liam McLaughlan, who has become one of the most sought-after speakers on the Left circuit.[108] It has attracted the former leader of the breakaway Scottish Labour Party of the 1970s, Jim Sillars, back into politics, through the Scottish Left Project which is exploring the possibility of forming a new political party to take a non-SNP left to the Scottish parliament in 2016.

The former SSP MSP Carolyn made a fairly obvious call for just such a party in a column in the *National* on 18th May 2015. She wrote:

Right now, there are thousands of folk across the social and geographical spectrum with a similar vision for a future independent Scotland. They are more critical of capitalism and the rule of big business. They want to go further than the SNP in wealth redistribution. They want essential areas of the economy, especially in the transport and energy sector, to be brought under public ownership and democratic control... So I think those on the progressive left have a responsibility to put something cohesive and credible together.

She pointed out that the various groupings that emerged from the referendum had lost traction and alluded to some of the controversies that had emerged over the ill-fated Yes Alliance after 2014. She also warned against repeating the experience of groups like Tommy Sheridan's Scottish Socialist Party. Leckie went on to say:

Anything that emerges cannot be dominated by any one individual or group. Its success lies in its ability to accommodate a range of ideas. Anything that tries to seize the ground by force of personality or by implementing a top-down, centralised, carbon copy of previous left incarnations will die at birth. It would need to be built with care and co-operation, trust and patience.

The Scottish Socialist Party and others have voted to set up a new party to fulfil this mission statement.[109] This 'Scotdemos', as it might be called, could not only occupy the space formally taken by the Scottish Socialist Party led by Tommy Sheridan, which once had six MSPs in the Scottish Parliament, it could also attract non-nationalist socialists from the ruins of the Scottish Labour Party. As argued in the previous chapter, there is no natural right for Scottish Labour to exist in its present form, except perhaps as a shell of its former self. Labour's inability to challenge the SNP leaves all of Scotland's political formations in a state of flux. If Labour is indeed succumbing to 'Pasokification', then a Scottish Syriza might be a real contender in the medium term in Scotland.

A ONE-PARTY STATE?

The Scottish Green party had a rather disappointing general election winning only 1% of the vote, though it will no doubt bounce back. The Greens are represented on the organisational committees of the Radical Independence Campaign but the party does not intend to be part of any new political party of the left. As one senior figure put it to me, 'rocks will melt in the sun' before they throw their lot in with the far Left. There is clearly a space in Scottish politics for a serious environmental party. Nicola Sturgeon has said very little about green issues since she has been in charge; her radicalism is largely about gender issues and social justice. She does not have the encyclopaedic knowledge of renewable energy that her predecessor Alex Salmond had. There is every possibility that the Greens could emerge as a serious opposition party in the Scottish Parliament in the future.

But for now, there really is only one political game in town and that is the Scottish National Party. In the end, the Yes Alliance simply couldn't find sufficient justification for its continued existence. Nicola Sturgeon's brand of nationalism is feminist and left-wing – at least in terms of rhetoric. The space for a non-aligned movement became narrower after she replaced Alex Salmond, a political leader who many believed – perhaps wrongly – was conservative in his political and economic thinking. And was also, very much, a male politician out of the old adversarial school.

The SNP has achieved the extraordinary trick of managing to colonise not just the centre but the centre left; not just nationalist politics but gender politics. It has a good track record on environmental issues, including the commitment to 80% reduction in greenhouse gas emissions by 2050. The Nationalists have also forged very strong links with the Scottish Trades Union Congress with whom they signed a Memorandum of Understanding on 15th May. The Scottish Trades Union Congress has never been formally affiliated to the Labour Party, but its statement made clear that the organisation was distancing itself from the Scottish Labour Party:

> The Government's commitment to reducing inequality alongside improving competitiveness, the creation of a Cabinet Secretary post for fair work, the establishment of a Fair Work Convention, the increase in Apprenticeships to 30,000 by 2020, the expansion of investment in union learning to £2.2 million a year, which will open up opportunities for leaning for over 9000 workers, are all a product of our constructive engagement with the Scottish Government and would not have happened had we been only interested in Labour.

But there is a problem here. Scotland may not be becoming a 'one-party state' as critics suggest – Scotland's parliament is elected on proportional representation which mitigates against one-party rule. But there is clearly a problem when the political opposition is in such disarray as it is now. The Scottish Liberal Democrats have almost ceased to exist and the Scottish Tories returned one of their worst shares of the Scottish vote ever. Labour has been all but wiped out. It is unfortunate that there is no broadly-based home rule movement which could attract non-nationalists.

There is also a pressing need for some kind of politics that begins to speak to the many middle class voters who may be intrigued by home rule but remain unconvinced of the virtues of Scottish independence, because they think the economic arguments are not soundly based. The SNP has some high profile business supporters, like Jim McColl of Clyde Blowers and Brian Souter of Stagecoach. But many, especially older middle class voters, feel that they are becoming excluded from representation in Scottish politics. This may seem a strange situation since, as earlier chapters indicated, the 56 new Scottish SNP MPs are mostly middle class themselves. But the party's rhetoric – if not always its policies, such as the freeze on council tax – seems oriented to the social democratic left and the working class, rather than to the people Labour leadership candidates call 'the aspirational'. Yet the truth is that if the Scottish nationalists are to win that second independence referendum, whenever it comes, the support of the sceptical middle classes is essential. Which is one reason why, as we will consider next, another referendum on independence may be some way off.

Chapter Six:

Independence of the mind

In the weeks after the 2015 General Election result in Scotland, there was a stunned silence from the UK political establishment. The predominantly Conservative UK press crowed over David Cameron's triumph over Ed Miliband and some even forecast the end of the Labour party as an electoral force. Labour politicians were equally gloomy with prominent MPs like John Cruddas saying that this was 'Labour's worst defeat since 1931' and that the party was now in a 'very dark place'.[110] Indeed, in Scotland it was arguably worse than in 1931. In the year the party split disastrously over Ramsay Macdonald's National Government, Labour at least won seven seats in Scotland. Now it has only one.

But press triumphalism was short-lived as the Westminster establishment began to reflect on the situation facing the UK. The unionist parties had been obliterated in Scotland. The Scottish Conservatives, even under the youthful and liberal-minded Ruth Davidson, had won their lowest share of the vote in over a century. The Liberal Democrats had been wiped from the Scottish mainland, its only MP Alistair Carmichael disgraced over lying about the 'Nikileaks' memo. No single party has ever won as many votes at a Scottish election or returned as high a proportion of seats as the SNP did in 2015.

Historically-minded commentators drew dark comparisons with Ireland. In 1918 the republican Sinn Féin won a comparable landslide in the days when Ireland was still part of the United Kingdom; though even its victory pales by comparison with the Scottish landslide achieved by the SNP. In the 1918 UK General Election, Sinn Féin returned only 73 out of Ireland's 105 seats.

Its MPs promptly withdrew from Westminster and prepared for secession and civil war. As the *Scotsman*'s Peter Jones remarked 'the precedent has some horrid political lessons for the main British political parties'.[111]

But perhaps not that horrid. Not only did the 56 Scottish National Party MPs not withdraw from Westminster, Nicola Sturgeon insisted that this unprecedented election victory was not even a mandate for another referendum on independence. She insisted that she 'respected' the outcome of the 2014 referendum and repeated her promise that only a 'material change in circumstances' would trigger another one. She cited the possibility of Scotland being forced out of the European Union as a result of a UK-wide referendum on British membership as being just such a material change. But she did not call for secession even when David Cameron appeared to rule out any future referendum on Scottish independence.[112]

The 56 MPs went south with a degree of dignity and even respect for the very Westminster parliament that they had condemned during the election campaign as damaging to Scotland. There was some elbowing with Labour MPs over who should sit where on the opposition benches and some un-parliamentary clapping in the Commons chamber, but there was no attempt to disrupt parliamentary procedures or make any gestures of defiance against the 'Imperial Parliament' as some Nationalists used to call Westminster. The SNP MPs swore their oath of allegiance to the Queen, despite many being republicans, and duly vowed to be responsible and diligent constituency representatives.

Which was all well and good. But the mere presence of this contingent of Scottish MPs in Westminster was a dramatic assertion that the current constitutional arrangements of the UK simply could not endure. As the Conservative writer Simon Heffer put it in the *New Statesman*, David Cameron and the unionists would 'have to accept, as they found it so hard to do a century ago with the Irish, that the tide of opinion for national self-determination in Scotland has strengthened appreciably since last September and that, with its 56 separatist seats, it has a new democratic legitimacy'.

Some Conservatives thought that, if the new Prime Minister David Cameron bided his time and made a few concessions, the Scottish MPs would get bored and frustrated and make mistakes. Westminster has a long history of absorbing and 'domesticating' radical elements by inviting them into the establishment. But this was to fail to understand the nature of the challenge facing Westminster. For not only had the unionists been wiped out in the Westminster parliament, there was also now a competing seat of democratic legitimacy in the Scottish Parliament four hundred miles away. Nicola Sturgeon would not be part of the Westminster village, and susceptible to its subtle blandishments.

This wasn't 'the worst crisis since the abdication' as Theresa May put it; it was actually much worse than that. The abdication of Edward VIII in 1935 posed no challenge to the integrity of the UK state. Scotland's comprehensive rejection of the unionist parties did. Things could not settle down to business as usual, however much the parliamentary authorities sought to welcome the SNP MPs to their new place of work. Apart from anything else, David Cameron had implicitly suggested that they were second-class citizens of the Westminster village by claiming that it would have been 'illegitimate' for those SNP MPs to vote down a Conservative Queen's Speech and provide support for a minority Labour government.

The fact that there has been no civil unrest accompanying the rise of nationalism in Scotland has perhaps led to a degree of complacency within Westminster. The press have been crying wolf for such a long time that they have lost any sense of how unnaturally calm the political climate in Scotland has been. Throughout the referendum campaign, London-based newspapers, and some Scottish ones too, ran stories about violent confrontations which were grossly exaggerated as well as inflammatory. There were references to 'aggressive nationalist thugs', 'hate-filled cybernats', 'gangs of abusive hecklers', and 'families divided by hatred'. In fact, by comparison with almost any previous nationalist movement in history, Scottish nationalism has almost been defined by its moderation and respect for the democratic process.

There has been no bomb-throwing ETA-style militants as in the Basque region of Spain. No mass demonstrations occupying city centres as in Catalonia or Greece. There has been no ethnic militias as in the former Yugoslavia, despite irresponsible politicians like the Labour Lord Robertson saying that independence for Scotland would lead to the 'Balkanisation' of Britain and 'Christmas for dictators'.[113] Not a single punch has been thrown during the events of 2014/15 in Scotland; not a single arrest; not a single broken window. The only missile thrown was one solitary egg, hurled at the Labour leader Jim Murphy during his 100 town speaking tour of Scotland during the 2014 referendum campaign. In the 2015 General Election not even an egg was hurled, though Jim Murphy did have a highly publicised verbal confrontation with the anti-cuts demonstrator Sean Clerkin and SNP hecklers at what became known as the 'Battle of St. Enoch's Square' in Glasgow on 4th May. But that only confirmed the extent to which Scotland's democratic uprising has been peaceful.

Consider the contrast with Ireland. The National Question there saw the violent Easter Rising of 1916 in Dublin by Irish nationalists, which was followed by bloody repression from the UK state. The 1918 election led to the eclipse of the Parnellite/Redmondite democratic Irish home rule party and a takeover by militant republicans. There was then a civil war with the British, followed by civil war between rival factions of Irish nationalists. Following partition and the creation of the Northern Ireland statelet, there was a further thirty year civil war in the province which lasted until 1998, leaving communities that are divided by hatred and enmity to this day. We can only be thankful, surely, that Scotland's uprising has been so peaceful.

When faced with provocation from the press or Tory MPs most Scottish nationalists have used social media to let off steam and provide an alternative network of communication to the unionist mainstream media.[114] The claims from Scottish unionist columnists, that Scottish voters had been seized by collective 'madness' were met with ridicule rather than rage.[115] Daft Twitter campaigns were invented to poke fun at the press as in #dollgate and at Tory ministers in #worstcrisissincetheabdication. Social media has been an important dimension of the Scottish independence movement. Despite the excesses of the abusive cybernats, it has been on the whole a moderating influence as well as a means of popular mobilisation.

Perhaps Scots' awareness of their own nation's history has also been a moderating influence: it has been a long and bloody one. Before the Act of Union in 1707, there were 400 years of almost continuous warfare with England. During the civil wars of the seventeenth century alone, as dynasties were toppled and restored, Scotland lost one tenth of its entire population in armed conflict. Then there were the Jacobite Rebellions of the eighteenth century which lowland Scots resisted often with as much determination as the English Hanoverians. If Scots seek the absence of war it is because they know that they are likely to come off worst.

We should also pay credit here to the responsibility of the UK government and of David Cameron himself for keeping the Scottish national question from boiling over. Unlike the Spanish state's rejection of Catalonia's independence referendum, the UK government signed the Edinburgh Agreement in 2012 and accepted the legality of the referendum on Scottish independence. Perhaps they would not have done so had they known how close the result would be but, nevertheless, even

Alex Salmond accepts that David Cameron played with 'a straight bat'. In the weeks immediately after the 2015 tsunami, David Cameron came north again to reassure Nicola Sturgeon that the result would be recognised and that there could be further powers devolved to Scotland than those contained in the proposed legislation to implement the Smith reforms.[116] She urged him to give Scotland responsibility over welfare, equalities, business taxes, employment law, and the minimum wage. These were not conceded by the UK government in the subsequent legislation implementing the so-called 'Vow', much to the dismay of the new SNP MPs.

But 'the most dangerous woman in Britain' also made clear she will have nothing to do with militant or unconstitutional attempts to achieve her goal of Scottish independence. She even suspended the SNP members who had participated in the rowdy heckling of the former Labour leader Jim Murphy, during the general election campaign. It must be the first time any party has actually disciplined members for shouting too loudly. Nor did she defend or seek to justify the behaviour of her Edinburgh South SNP candidate Neil Hay, when it was alleged that he had said offensive things on the Internet.

BOILING THE FROG

European observers often wonder at the quiescence of the Scottish independence movement, given the turbulent history of nationalist struggles elsewhere in the UK and abroad. The absence of big colourful street demonstrations is something that puzzles foreign journalists, especially those from Eastern Europe and Spain. Where's the righteous anger? Where's the passion? The answer to this is simple: the Scots don't go out on the streets because thus far, at any rate, the nationalists have found – to paraphrase a Sinn Fein slogan – that the ballot box really is more effective than the Armalite. The Scots restored their parliament after 300 years without a shot being fired. It was a result of years of civic action around the cross-party Scottish Constitutional Convention after its Declaration of Sovereignty in 1989. The referendum of 1997 could be seen as a trial run for the 2015 landslide, as Scots quietly but decisively voted three to one in favour of restoring their parliament. They also eliminated the UK's party of government, the Conservatives, at the 1997 General Election.

The Scottish Parliament could have been a toothless talking shop, a 'pretendy parliament' as Billy Connolly styled it, but it wasn't. The late Labour Scottish Secretary and first First Minister Donald Dewar deserves honourable mention for his ingenious drafting of the Scotland Act of 1998 which established Holyrood. The legislation avoided specifying the powers of the Scottish Parliament and only laid down those which were reserved to Westminster like currency, defence, broadcasting, etc. As Dewar said himself, this made devolution 'a process not an event' because the Scottish Parliament was able to extend its powers without needing future referendums. The concurrent Sewel convention asserted that no act of the UK Parliament could be imposed on Holyrood against its will. This was a massive advance in political autonomy. When you have a national legislature, elected on proportional representation and with primary law making powers, you are already 80% of the way to self-government. After a few years of indifferent Holyrood governance, the Scottish voters lost faith with Labour. It had performed, if you like, its historic task. The country was looking for a more demonstrative form of political representation that would take devolution to the next level. They found it in the form of the 2007-11 minority SNP administration, which many, including Nicola Sturgeon, believe showed Holyrood at its best.[117]

But the success of the Scottish Parliament in managing domestic legislation in Scotland, on issues like smoking, the elimination of private provision from the NHS, and the abolition of tuition fees, raised the question of economic autonomy. Could the Scottish Parliament continue to be funded on what was, effectively, a hand-out from Westminster in the form of the annual Barnett Formula? It was a former Labour leader again, Wendy Alexander, who effectively set the stage for fiscal devolution with the 2008/9 Calman Commission. This made the case for devolution max, though perhaps Professor Calman didn't realise it at the time, for the form of partial income tax devolution he recommended was quickly set aside.[118] Calman argued that for reasons of transparency, accountability, fairness, and responsibility the Scottish Parliament needed to raise its own revenues. These principles were even adopted by the Conservatives' own Strathclyde Commission on the future governance of Scotland in 2014.[119] In retrospect, the Calman Commission made fiscal autonomy all but inevitable. Once you have won the argument that a national parliament needs financial responsibility it is difficult to argue that it should only be partially responsible. Where do you stop?

This may seem a somewhat teleological account of Scotland's progress to independence. It makes it sound as if the Scottish voters and politicians always in some way knew where they were going – and of course they didn't. History is not written in advance. But I think it is a useful way to comprehend what has finally happened in 2014/15 and why it has happened. This is not an isolated episode; it is the conclusion of a long process through which Scotland has gradually re-appropriated national autonomy. You might even imagine it as the constitutional equivalent of boiling a frog: if you turn it up too fast, it will jump out of the pan. But if you turn the heat up gradually, imperceptibly, the frog will boil without knowing what has hit it.

DELIVER US FROM EVEL

Of course, this constitutional frog could boil over at any moment. The current situation – as Sir Tom Devine has remarked – represents the greatest threat to the Union since 1707.[120] The next few years could be crucial in maintaining the stable state within which Scotland is renegotiating its place in the Union. The Sewel Convention is likely to be tested in the course of this parliament, as the most right-wing Conservative government since the days of Margaret Thatcher tries to implement measures like the abolition of the Human Rights Act which is opposed by Holyrood. The 2017 referendum on British membership of Europe and the imposition of English Votes for English Laws could each trigger a further crisis. And there will be continued wrangling over the Barnett Formula on Scottish spending.

The First Minister Nicola Sturgeon had made clear that any attempt to force Scotland out of Europe against its will would be considered a *casus belli* for another independence referendum.[121] However, this was always going to be a rather rocky terrain on which to fight the next stage of independence. For a start, it was never entirely clear that Scots were particularly enthusiastic about the European Union. Certainly, Scots have never indicated that leaving it is any kind of priority and opinion polls suggest a clear majority would vote to stay in Europe, but not by all that much.[122] With nearly nine tenths of the population, England was always going to claim that its views should predominate in any UK-wide referendum.

Nevertheless, the SNP is right to argue that if the UK really were a 'family of nations' and had a federal constitution like Canada or America, then the state parliaments in Scotland, Wales, and Northern Ireland might indeed have expected a veto on such a great constitutional issue as membership of the EU. There have been various attempts to kick-start a federal restructuring of the UK, including the Labour Peer Lord Foulkes' Campaign for Federalism.[123] It has been suggested that the Conservative's 'Northern Powerhouse' programme, devolving spending power to northern English city-regions like Manchester, is a step in a federal direction. But as David Torrance, the *Herald* columnist and author of *Britain Rebooted: Why Federalism Would Be Good for the Nations and Regions of the UK* has argued, turning the House of Lords into a directly elected Senate 'is the key' to any serious federalisation.[124] Yet reform of the Upper House was effectively shelved by the Tories in their 2015 election manifesto as 'not a priority'. The Conservatives have opposed any revisiting of electoral reform and certainly do not propose to set up directly elected English regional assemblies. When the London Mayor Boris Johnson cries 'federalism', he is meaning something altogether different.

The Conservatives seem determined to press ahead with English Votes for English Laws, which might be called the federalism of fools. Simply removing full voting rights from certain categories of MP in the House of Commons is not coherent constitutional reform, and is more like a punitive expedition against the opposition Labour Party. Barring Scottish MPs from voting on nominally English affairs in an unreformed unitary parliament could create huge instability. It seems mainly designed to ensure that a future Labour government cannot credibly seek office on the back of the votes of Scottish Labour MPs. The fact that these are now thin on the ground is beside the point.

EVEL is incoherent because you cannot have a parliament in which all elected members are accorded equivalence, and then bar some of them from voting on certain bills. Only the creation of a de facto English parliament could achieve that legislative right. The SNP have said that they will not vote on non-Scottish issues as a measure of respect. But in a unitary parliament there is always going to be a temptation for Scottish MPs to vote on moral issues, such as fox-hunting in England (even though it is already banned in Scotland), on the grounds that it is a UK parliament they are voting in, not a devolved English one.

Three Irish Home Rule bills attempted to resolve the conundrum of how to have regional voting in a unitary parliament, what we now call the West Lothian Question, and they failed. Lloyd George looked at attempts to get the Speaker of the Commons to certify certain bills as exclusively English in which Irish MPs would be excluded. This was the so-called 'In-and-Out' method. But it proved impossible to find an adequate definition of what an exclusively English bill is. Apparently English measures often have a financial impact on other parts of the UK through budgetary mechanisms. The NHS is a case in point: market reforms can have a financial impact on Scotland through the Barnett Formula.

But the Conservatives intend to press ahead with a form of EVEL which attempts to give English MPs an effective veto on English bills. They are proposing to exclude Scottish MPs from certain measures in the budget. There is to be an English rate of tax for example, which will be voted on by English MPs.[125] The opposition parties have said that this would be unacceptable and would be contrary to the promises made in the Smith Commission. But it has to be said that, from an English point of view, this will seem an inevitable concomitant of Scotland having its own devolved tax powers.

The moral case for England to have control of its laws is unanswerable; but the mechanism has yet to be found that can achieve this within a unitary sovereign parliament. In the absence of a resolution of this constitutional contradiction, the complaints in the UK press that Scotland is somehow privileged in the UK system can only grow. Yet a federal solution to this problem seems as distant as ever, not least because there seems to be no demand for it in England, the dominant partner in the Union. This constitutional push me pull you is generating tensions that can only further weaken Scotland's links to the

United Kingdom's parliament.

FOLLOWING THE MONEY

In politics it always makes sense to follow the money, and it may well be financial issues that precipitate the crisis that finally leads to the dissolution of the UK as we know it. The Smith proposals are, it is commonly agreed, a hastily thought-out rag bag of measures, a 'shambles' according to the former Labour First Minister, Jack McConnell.[126] Scotland is to get powers to vary income tax bands, though not the personal allowance. Nor is Scotland to have power over national insurance, VAT, excise duties, corporation tax, and such like. Since income tax is an increasingly minor tax but also highly visible and politically sensitive (increases in income tax are to be made illegal under the UK government proposals) it is going to be a very unstable foundation upon which to build a fiscally-responsible, transparent, and accountable Scottish Parliament. The Scottish Parliament has had powers to raise income tax by 3p in the pound since 1999 and has never used them.

But the implementation of Smith will make the Barnett Formula redundant. Not overnight, perhaps, but it will end the system through which Scotland receives annual increases in public spending linked, by a fixed formula, to increases in spending in the UK as a whole. For years academics and politicians have been saying that the Barnett Formula is past its sell-by date. This is surely the moment when it is finally thrown in the bin. During the referendum campaign, Jim Murphy insisted on saying that he would support the Barnett Formula 'now, tomorrow, forever', but most authorities believe that if it still exists at all, Barnett will account for barely one third of Scottish spending by 2020.[127] There is no longer a fiscal status quo.

This will leave open the question of how the Scottish Parliament is to be financed. The Nationalists' proposals for what they now call 'full fiscal responsibility' are intentionally vague – and now assumed to take place over a number of years rather than overnight. This has led to an assumption by some commentators that the Scottish government is backing away from full fiscal autonomy because it would lead to a £7.6bn shortfall in spending, according to the Institute for Fiscal Studies.[128] But these are regarded by the SNP as tendentious calculations, and the Nationalists continue to believe that, even with a fluctuating oil price, Scotland can still manage its own financial affairs over time. The Institute for Fiscal Studies, they say, is the old 'too poor, too wee, too stupid' argument in statistical form.

What most Nationalists appear to mean by fiscal responsibility is something similar to the arrangements in the Basque Country of Spain, where the regional government pays a contribution or 'percept' for common services such as defence, central administration, foreign affairs, and suchlike. This, they say, is a different kind of fiscal autonomy to the tax devolution assumed by the Institute for Fiscal Studies. There is a fairly obvious precedent for this in the UK's own recent history: the Irish Home Rule bills of the last century provided the original model for 'devolution max'. Ireland was expected to be self-financing and would pay an agreed sum of its revenues to what was then called the 'Imperial Parliament' in Westminster to cover the cost of things like defence and foreign affairs. This is, of course, a highly politicised calculation. Scotland would clearly not wish, for example, to pay the cost of new Trident nuclear submarines.

The SNP's critics insist that the collapse of the oil price has ruined Scotland's prospects and that Full Fiscal Autonomy would involve tax increases, or radical public spending cuts, to meet the notional deficit. The Nationalists have conceded that the taxes probably would rise on higher incomes and the mansion tax. There is an interesting parallel here with Irish history. Between the Second Irish Home Rule Bill of 1893 and the Third in 1912, Ireland's fiscal position deteriorated largely because of the introduction of the welfare state in 1909. Irish finances would have been in severe deficit if the Imperial Contribution had been set at the fixed amount proposed in 1893 when Ireland was in surplus. According to Professor Vernon Bogdanor in *Devolution in the United Kingdom*, the assumption in 1912 was that there might even have to be a REVERSE contribution to Ireland from the UK Exchequer, at least for a time, to prevent a catastrophic increase in Irish taxes to pay for old age pensions.[129]

The Third Irish Home Rule Bill was passed but never implemented because of the First World War and the Easter Rising, so we will never know if this would have been acceptable to the English taxpayer. But the point is: full fiscal autonomy is never quite as straightforward or autonomous as it seems. It involves continuing negotiation. In all federal or quasi-federal arrangements, richer states are required to help less well off states through financial transfers calculated by what is usually called an 'equalisation formula'. As the SNP MP George Kerevan has argued, this would almost certainly apply under FFA.[130] However, there is no guarantee that the equalisation will necessarily mean transfer payments to Scotland. Indeed, during the years of oil wealth, Scotland might have been called upon to make finance transfers to support less well advantaged regions in the rest of the UK under FFA. Even now, Scotland is the third richest region of the UK in terms of GDP per head after London and the South East of England.

This is all horribly complex and that is one reason why the SNP believe independence is preferable to federalism. In addition to financial transfers there is also the question of what debt the Scottish government would be able to take on under fiscal autonomy. That would involve negotiation both on the acceptable level of Scottish National Debt and Scotland's share of the UK debt pile. The UK government has ruled out FFA so the argument appears somewhat academic. Nevertheless, in the longer term, it seems that something like devolution max – for all its difficulties – may now be inevitable, if only to address the clamour from sections of the UK press for an end to the Barnett Formula and to prevent Scots from accessing English tax payers' money. Fiscal autonomy does at least have the merit of being easy to understand, reasonably fair, relatively transparent, and a little more responsible. Though before long, both sides may start to look back with fond nostalgia to the days of the Barnett Formula which, for all its faults, actually delivered fairly stable funding increases for nearly four decades.

REFERENDUM OR NEVERENDUM

Support for independence appears to be growing. In the aftermath of the general election, opinion polls indicated that a majority of Scots under the age of sixty are now supporters of independence.[131] This has inevitably led to calls from some SNP supporters for Nicola Sturgeon to demand another independence referendum. But my reading of the SNP leader's mind is that she is not in any hurry, and for a very good reason. An early referendum is unlikely to lead to a very different result from 18th September 2014. Assuming the UK government repeats its refusal to contemplate a currency union, then all the financial horrors of 'Project Fear' would be rolled out once again. The reality is that without goodwill from the larger partner in the Union, an independent Scotland's life could be made very difficult, especially in the early years.

As in 2014, businesses would threaten to leave because of 'currency instability'. The Bank of England would refuse to be lender of last resort, which means that the rating agencies would mark down Scotland's credit rating, which means higher borrowing costs etc. There is no doubt that Scotland with its many economic advantages could become a viable independent country like Norway or Denmark – even David Cameron has accepted that. But the problem is all about getting from here to there, and persuading the cautious Scottish middle classes that it would be worth the hassle. There will always be imponderables, insecurities, and an implicit threat from the rest of the UK to act in such a way as to wreck an independent Scotland's economy.

This makes overnight separation a hard sell. The currency 'diktat', as the SNP called George Osborne's 2014 Declaration on the Pound, in my view undermined the moral basis of the Union and destroyed for many Scots the illusion that it was a partnership. But that doesn't mean that Scottish voters will want to take the risk of separation if it looks likely to lead to economic ruin. It is for this reason that the Scottish National Party had for nearly two decades, under the guidance of Alex Salmond, effectively parked formal independence as a long-term aspiration, while getting on with the business of governing Scotland day to day. This is a kind of 'independence of the mind', as it has been called by the Scottish writer, Gerry Hassan: behaving as if Scotland were already an independent country, whatever the constitutional reality.[132] Keeping on, keeping on.

Nicola Sturgeon is very good at this independent mindfulness, as she has demonstrated on the international stage during visits such as her outing in America in June 2015. She swapped jokes with Jon Stewart on the Daily Show; met officials in the White House; lectured foreign affairs think tanks and generally behaved as if she had every right to be there representing Scotland. The diplomatic response was to the effect that she is someone that the White House could do business with – if it had to.[133] Alex Salmond never mastered this apparently effortless statesmanship. He was a politician from a different age, when his party was on the margins and its leaders had to fight to get attention. Anyone who thought that Nicola Sturgeon would be permanently in his shadow has had to think again.

In a sense Nicola Sturgeon has reversed the independence strategy of Sinn Féin. When they won their landslide in 1918 the Sinn Féiners immediately withdrew from any cooperation with the old imperial state. Nicola Sturgeon has, by contrast, insisted that she wants constructive engagement with Westminster. She even proposed supporting a government of the very same unionist Labour party that had ruled out any currency union with an independent Scotland. Some observers suspect that Nicola Sturgeon has given up on independence altogether, that her 'utilitarian nationalism' sees no need for it, provided social objectives are realised. I don't believe that is the case.

However, in my view, another independence referendum will require not only a 'material change' in relations between Holyrood and Westminster, but also an unequivocal demand for a referendum by the Scottish people. Only if the opinion polls are showing a sustained and substantial lead – over 60% for Yes – would a referendum on independence be likely to succeed. At the time of writing, Yes is still running at about 48-49% even though the SNP's popularity continues to increase.[134] I suspect myself that, it will be some years before another referendum happens, and that if and when it does, the SNP will be looking to have a decisive result that mirrors the 2015 General Election. This does not, however, mean that Scots need to settle back into a curmudgeonly unionism in the meantime – they will continue to live as if they are 'in the early days of a better nation', to use the indyref cliché. Scotland is already living in a very different political culture to that which exists south of the border in terms of attitudes to matters like welfare, immigration, Europe, and taxation. There remains no party of the political right in Scotland. There is nothing to stop Scots following their leader in behaving as if they were already

Denmark. What you think is what you become, as self-help gurus say.

SCOTLAND'S PEACEFUL REVOLUTION

Any lingering doubts about the fundamental change that has taken place in Scotland's attitude to the Union must surely have been dispelled by the result of the 2015 General Election. Scotland is now a different country and the United Kingdom a part of history. The Union was a great achievement for its time and – the abortive '45 Rebellion aside – ended military conflict forever between Scotland and England.[135] And for most of the next 300 years, Scots were content to be junior partners in the United Kingdom. In the days of Empire, Scotland did rather well out of being part of Britain – certainly by comparison with what had gone before. The middle classes, who were the only people who counted in the nineteenth century, were solidly committed to Empire, though they voted Liberal rather than Conservative.

After the Second World War, Scots – now enfranchised – remained enthusiastic members of the United Kingdom, but it was now the UK that introduced the welfare state, the NHS, and regional industrial policies. Scotland had willingly handed over its oil wealth to the UK exchequer believing it would be used for the common good. But from 1979 onwards, Scotland began to realise that it was no longer part of the same social democratic enterprise. The Empire had long gone. The Postwar Settlement was scrapped and Britain transformed through the economics of neoliberalism.

Industry collapsed, the poll tax was introduced, a new and rapacious form of capitalism emerged based on financial services in the city of London. The old bargain was clearly no longer in operation; the caring sharing union of Labour imagination seemed an illusion. This was a devil-take-the-hindmost union in which whoever grabbed the most got the most. Scots began to feel they had donated their hydrocarbon wealth to a cause that no longer deserved it. In its post-imperial adventures, the new UK seemed alien too. During the Iraq war, perhaps for the first time in two centuries, Scots found they could not support a conflict in which British soldiers were dying.

Scots may have been deluding themselves that they were in a partnership with the rest of the UK – they often got the worst deal on the battlefield or in the colonial administration – but that is what most Scots genuinely believed and it was a delusion that lasted a long time. But the basis for that partnership is clearly over. As the writer Neal Ascherson put it a few days after the general election:

As a piece of architecture, [the Union] was abandoned in 1999, when the devolved Scottish Parliament met. Rain blew in as the slates fell off; pews were looted; and the Holyrood elections of 2007 and 2011 brought down more of the roof. Last week, Alex Salmond said he heard the Scottish lion roaring. I heard the rumble as the union's floor gave way and fell into the crypt.[136]

Dismantling the architecture of the 300 year-old Union need not necessarily lead to conflict. Scots are not oppressed people and do not live in a colony. They are not under English or British tyranny, despite what some of the '45 Group' of radical nationalists claim, and have full democratic and civil rights (subject, of course, to the plans to abolish the Human Rights Act). This is an important reason why the kind of militant politics that people normally associate with revolutions has been absent in Scotland.

Of course, revolutions, even democratic ones, can get nasty. Eventually people lose patience. Confrontation becomes easier than comprehension. We've seen the dark side with the cybernats calling Labour 'red Tory scum' and the unitrolls calling the SNP 'fascist scum'. So long as it stays on the Internet and doesn't spill onto the streets, this bile will be tolerable, if demeaning to both sides. Those in the middle will have singular responsibility to try to prevent these antagonisms – which are inevitable when such important matters are at stake – from straying beyond the bounds of civilised debate.

However, there has been a challenge to the ideological hegemony of the old order. The most obvious sign is that at least half of the Scottish voters no longer believe much of what they read in the mainstream press or hear on TV. As someone who works in the 'mainstream media', it is a matter of some concern to me that the UK and Scottish press and the BBC seem largely in denial about this breach of trust. Many journalists and unionist politicians seem to think the Scottish voters have just been badly advised. Don't they realise that the SNP is a nationalist cult? I hear them say. What do flags matter anyway?

Many think the case for remaining in the union is so obvious that the voters must have lost their reason not to realise it. Why risk losing out by many billions a year? Why not accept the beneficence of the (residual) Barnett Formula and have an easy life? But this is rather like the parent mystified when the son or daughter decides to leave home with all its comforts and security. Eventually, when people or nations decide they want to run their own affairs, you just have to let them. Telling them they aren't up to it, that they'd end up in penury, only makes them more determined.

The road ahead is clear. There will now be heated arguments about how to reform and ultimately replace the Barnett Formula, and how Scotland should pay for common services, until eventually some form of full fiscal responsibility will be introduced. Whether this causes financial hardship in Scotland is impossible to judge. It depends on the terms under which tax autonomy is granted, the value of hydrocarbon resources, and the size of Scotland's continuing contribution to the UK. But the issue is no longer fiscal or even economic, but a question of political autonomy. The unmistakable message of the 2015 General Election is that Scotland is minded to complete the repatriation of political and economic autonomy begun by the devolution process. The Barnett comfort blanket is no more. Scots will have to be free to make their own mistakes.

But if and when independence arrives, as seems inevitable now, some ties with the United Kingdom will remain. Alex Salmond has said as much, by calling for Scotland to retain the Union of the Crowns of 1603. The 2013 Independence White Paper makes clear that Scots could still describe themselves as 'British' after independence. It is geographically impossible anyway for Scotland to separate from England on this small island off the European mainland. There is always going to be a range of common problems – from relations with Europe to marine conservation; from immigration to energy policy; broadcasting to defence cooperation – upon which the two countries are going to have to cooperate. I would not even put it beyond the bounds of possibility that Scots might continue to send representatives to Westminster after independence. After all, if many important decisions on matters like interest rates and energy subsidies are to continue to be made in London, it makes sense to have some representation there. If and when Scotland becomes independent it will still send MEPs and financial contributions to the European Union, so why not the UK union?

And there is still that remote possibility that a new UK constitution could be devised that could accommodate Scottish ambitions without a formal declaration of independence by Scotland. There might be a sudden flash of constitutional imagination. A UK constitutional convention might be convened which enlists the brightest minds in the country to square the circle. After all, we did break the Enigma code. But failing that, I can see no better solution than for Scotland simply to be an independent country, still part of the UK but in a very different relationship.

There might even be a grand compromise, in the best British tradition. Scotland and the rest of the UK might decide that that there is no point in continuing with piecemeal constitutional wrangling and that the simplest solution is to negotiate an amicable separation. This has happened many times before in British history. When Canada, the Irish Free State, and Australia became self-governing eighty years ago, it turned out to be surprisingly straightforward. The UK Parliament simply passed the Statute of Westminster on December 11th 1931 saying that it would no longer legislate for those 'dominions'.[137] Who knows, history may repeat itself. The United Kingdom could engineer a velvet divorce, after which Scotland and England keep calm and carry on in a new UK with the Queen still as Head of State. It would be a very British solution to this very Scottish national revolution.

But make no mistake: Scotland would be an independent country.

Postscript:

The Empire Strikes Back

The General Election of 2015 may have seen the most dramatic result in Scottish history, but any thoughts that the SNP's success might lead to an early change of heart by Westminster, let alone progress towards the mythical goal of federalism, were quickly dispelled. The governing UK Conservative party did appear briefly to take a fresh look at devolution max and Full Fiscal Autonomy. Indeed, the senior Conservative MP Edward Leigh made a rather impressively open-minded speech on the first day of the Scotland Bill debate in June 2015. He argued that the UK should heed the lessons of Irish Home Rule, devolve all oil revenues and tax powers to Holyrood, and continue to subsidise the Scottish Parliament if necessary to meet any shortfall in funding that might result from the abolition of the Barnett Formula.[138]

This was somewhat in advance of what the SNP themselves were calling for. Their convoluted amendment to the Scotland Bill called only for progress towards Full Fiscal Autonomy rather than its immediate introduction. It proposed that Scotland and the rest of the UK should enter into an 'Economic Agreement' in which the two governments would 'over a period of time [...] establish a plan [and] [...] coordinate their economic and fiscal policies in the context of Full Fiscal Autonomy'.[139] This looked to many people rather like the sinner who wanted to be made pure 'but not yet Lord, not yet'. The economic context of this debate, and in particular the collapse of the oil price by 50%, clearly had a bearing on the SNP's enthusiasm for making the Scottish Parliament fully reliant on its own funding. Though the Nationalists insisted that they had not given up on their manifesto pledge on 'fiscal responsibility' as they now called it. It was never meant to be an overnight affair.

There was also a fitful debate about the meaning of the 'no detriment' principle set out in the Smith Commission Report of November 2014. In a column in *The National*, the former leader of the Scottish National Party, Alex Salmond, suggested that no detriment meant that the Scottish Government should not suffer any loss as a result of the decline in oil prices, and that the £7bn 'black hole' in the Scottish accounts identified by the Institute for Fiscal Studies – arising from fiscal autonomy – would be a joint responsibility of the UK. 'Why would anyone moan', wrote the newly elected MP for Gordon, 'about financial changes which left neither Scotland nor Westminster worse off or better off?'[140] Needless to say, Labour disputed this interpretation of the Smith Commission's provisions. They claimed that, under Full Fiscal Autonomy, Scotland would have to meet the cost of any budgetary shortfall through increasing taxes or cuts in public spending. This is an impossible argument to resolve in the abstract. All federal systems involve financial transfers between richer and poorer states. The question is whether Full Fiscal Autonomy would be compatible with federalism or would be de facto independence. That is a political question rather than a narrowly fiscal one.

But these preliminary exchanges were largely academic anyway because the UK Prime Minister, David Cameron, had made clear within days of the general election that the UK government would not entertain any version of full fiscal autonomy or devomax for the Scottish Parliament. Indeed, the government rejected all the amendments placed by the SNP to the Scotland Bill, including its calls for control of the minimum wage, employment law, and welfare policy to be devolved. The Scottish Secretary, Scotland's sole Tory MP David Mundell, promised to 'listen' to the arguments made by the opposition parties. But a legislative red line was firmly drawn under the devolution process at the reforms contained in the Smith Commission, even though it had reported long before the general election and despite the fact that the Prime Minister, on his visit to Scotland shortly after election day, had suggested that further devolution was on the cards.[141] But the Scottish Secretary David Mundell insisted that the government had only committed itself to implement Smith in full.

TAXING QUESTIONS

The Scotland Bill 2015 proposed to hand the Scottish Parliament full powers to vary levels and bands of income tax (though not personal allowances); assignment of one half of VAT revenue; and powers to increase certain welfare benefits 'in agreement' with the UK government. There was a somewhat sterile debate about whether or not this latter constituted a 'veto' on the Scottish Parliament's powers over welfare. The new special adviser to the Scottish Secretary, Professor Adam Tomkins of Glasgow University, told the Scottish government to stop 'bleating' about alleged vetoes. He said that Holyrood would have all the powers it needed to enhance benefits, and if there were any disputes, 'then there's a neutral arbiter in the form of the courts'.[142]

The government's intention was clarified by David Cameron during Prime Minister's Questions on July 1st 2015. In answer to a question from the SNP Westminster leader, Angus Robertson, he replied:

> Let me tell him again: instead of endlessly talking about the process, is it not time that the SNP started to talk about how they are going to use these powers? Why do they not tell us? Which welfare benefits do

they want to put up? Which taxes do they want to increase? Why do they not start to tell us?[143]

Clearly, David Cameron had decided to make no further legislative concessions to the SNP but instead to try to hoist the Scottish government on its own fiscal petard. The UK government wanted to give the Scottish Parliament just enough powers to raise taxes in order to mitigate the £12bn cuts in benefits introduced by the 2015 UK Welfare Bill and Finance Bill. This would force the SNP to put its money where its mouth is. The UK government also wanted to highlight the fact that the Chancellor intended to pass a law to freeze income tax, VAT, and national insurance until 2020. This would allow the Scottish Conservatives – in this scheme – to return to electoral acceptability in Scotland as the party of low taxation.[144]

If the Scottish Conservatives believed that this would make them popular overnight they were wrong. After all, the new tax powers would not be introduced until 2019 at the earliest. In the meantime, the new Scottish rate of income tax – product of the previous Scotland Bill 2012 and introduced in April 2016 – would give little more latitude to increase top taxes than the original powers of the 1998 Scotland Act. The Scottish Parliament has always had the power to vary the basic rate of income tax up or down by 3p in the pound. This Scottish Variable Rate has never been used. The Scotland Act 2012 gave Holyrood the further power to vary the first 10 percentage points of income tax (thought not dividend and other forms of saving and investment income). But it only gave Parliament the power to vary all bands simultaneously. In other words, there was little scope here to make the tax regime more progressive by increasing the upper rates while keeping the basic rate unchanged. The assessment of many tax experts, therefore, was that there would be very little change after the implementation of the 2012 Act in April 2016.[145] The Scottish political parties of the left tend to talk a great deal about progressive taxation – Labour MPs often claim that the Scottish government's council tax freeze is regressive – but they have never actually increased them, despite having had the power to do so since 1999. Neither the SNP nor Labour has gone into a recent election promising to lift the cap on council tax, and nor has either party ever seriously proposed using the Scottish Variable Rate.

It is safe to say that Scottish voters were left unmoved by these arcane and technical debates about taxation and by the succession of Scotland Acts, which seemed to be emerging from the legislative process like London buses. Few Scots probably grasped the distinction between the 2012 and 2015 Scotland Acts, and the political parties didn't appear to be very sure either. As with Full Fiscal Autonomy, most of the complex arguments about the impact of the new tax regimes went over the heads of the electorate.

NATIONALISM HAD NOTHING TO DO WITH IT

What voters did notice was the increased presence of Scottish MPs in Westminster. The 56 Nationalist MPs may not have had the numbers to decide legislation, but they exploited the theatre of politics to great effect. Westminster is the greatest stage in politics and some new stars were soon treading the boards. The most successful was the twenty-year-old MP for Paisley and Renfrewshire South, Mhairi Black, who had broken Labour hearts by defeating the former Foreign Secretary Douglas Alexander. Her maiden speech on 15th July, citing Tony Benn as her political inspiration, was viewed more than ten million times on the Internet within a week and won plaudits from across the political spectrum – even though few agreed with her arguments.[146]

Actually, her speech raised a few eyebrows in Nationalists circles too, for its conflation of the politics of independence with the politics of social democracy. She said:

> The SNP did not triumph on a wave of nationalism, in fact nationalism has nothing to do with what has happened in Scotland. We triumphed on a wave of hope – hope that we could have an alternative to the wave of Thatcherite neoliberal policies from this chamber. [...] Like so many SNP members I come from a traditional socialist, Labour family. Like so many, I feel that it is the Labour party that left me, not the other way about.[147]

This could have been interpreted as marginalising the raison d'etre of the Scottish National Party, which is after all the party of national independence. Black's speech also raised the question of whether, if the Labour party were to 'come back' to people like her, they would necessarily remain in the Scottish National Party. It was a striking illustration of the dichotomy between 'utilitarian nationalism' and 'existential nationalism', which I examined in earlier chapters of this book. Is the SNP essentially a social democratic party or a nationalist one? Is there a contradiction between the two? If a genuine social democratic party was to be elected to Westminster, would that render Scottish independence unnecessary? This was to become a live issue later that very month, as a certain Bennite Labour politician began transforming the political culture of the UK Labour Party.

But for the time being, the SNP MPs had the left field largely to themselves in Westminster. Indeed, after Labour abstained in the vote on the government's Welfare Reform and Work Bill which sought to curb tax credits and cut £12bn from benefits, the 56 SNP MPs physically occupied the Labour benches in the Commons Chamber arguing that they were now the only real opposition in parliament.[148] They said that if Labour had joined them in the division lobbies, the Tory bill could have been defeated – though the arithmetic was probably against them here since the Conservatives had a twelve seat overall majority in the Commons. However, the vote would certainly have been close. It would have taken only a handful of rebels to defeat the flagship bill. In the event, forty-eight Labour MPs rebelled against their leadership and voted against the bill. Labour front benchers like the leadership contender Andy Burnham said afterwards that they regretted abstaining and that the vote had been a 'mess'. Few disagreed.

There will be debate for many years over the extent to which the SNP helped ignite the conflagration in the UK Labour Party that led to the surprise landslide victory of Jeremy Corbyn as leader. But there is little doubt that the SNP played a part, at least by example, through their forthright conduct in parliament in the months immediately following the 2015 General Election. The SNP had, of course, invited Labour to form a post-election 'progressive alliance' in Westminster, based on opposition to austerity cuts, renewal of Trident, and welfare reforms. But the then Labour leadership had been uninterested in any form of overt cooperation with the Nationalists, whom many blamed for contributing to Labour's election defeat. Initially, the UK Labour leadership tried – like David Cameron – to ignore the SNP's Westminster contingent. They believed that Scottish voters would eventually become disillusioned with their lack of influence on UK politics. After all, there were only 56 of them out of a Westminster parliament of 650. The SNP had also declined to be represented in the House of Lords, where many of the important constitutional provisions of the Scotland Bill were likely to be debated and amended. Some Labour MPs sought to turn against them the same 'feeble fifty' jibe used by the SNP against Labour in the 1990s.[149] Initially, the SNP appeared to be playing to the script and resorting to what was described as childish attention-seeking: flouting Commons tradition over seating arrangements and clapping in the debating chamber. However, the SNP MPs were not so easy to dismiss and they soon managed to punch well above their weight.

SHOOTING THE TORY FOX

As the third largest party in the UK, the SNP had the right to be called more regularly in debates and to be represented in parliamentary committees. One of the most extraordinary, almost surreal, moments for those of us who have been following Scottish politics in recent decades was the sight of an SNP MP Pete Wishart becoming chair of the Scottish Affairs Select Committee. Under its previous Labour chair, Ian Davidson, the Scottish Select had been one of the leading edges of Westminster unionism, producing reports condemning the economics of independence. Davidson, who lost his Govan seat in the May tsunami, had even described the SNP in 2011 as 'neo-fascists'. But it wasn't only in presentational terms that the 56 MPs were making an impact. They also appeared to be having a significant legislative impact too, on issues like fox hunting and English Votes for English Laws (EVEL).

The SNP abandoned its self-denying ordinance against voting on matters like fox hunting, which could reasonably be described as of exclusive interest only to voters in England. Hunting with hounds has long been outlawed by the Scottish Parliament where English MPs are, of course, unrepresented. David Cameron wanted to repeal the 2004 legislation banning fox hunting in England and, quite reasonably, expected the

56 Nationalists to abstain. After all, on account of the West
Lothian Question, Nicola Sturgeon had herself once cited fox
hunting as one of the issues on which it was not legitimate for
Scottish MPs to vote in Westminster. In February 2015 she
said: 'The SNP have a longstanding position of not voting on
matters that purely affect England – such as fox-hunting south
of the border, for example – and we stand by that.'

The SNP leader justified her commitment on the grounds
that the UK Conservatives had refused to recognise the result
of the general election in Scotland and had rejected all the
SNP's amendments to the Scotland Bill. She said she wanted
to 'send a message' that Scotland could not be ignored. She
was accused by the Prime Minister of 'opportunism' which was
manifestly justified.[150] But it was rather effective opportunism.
The government had to cancel the vote on fox hunting for fear
of losing it. There are a number of opponents of fox hunting
on the Conservative benches and many concluded that the
SNP's action would make it impossible to repeal the 2004 Fox
Hunting Act.

The SNP was widely criticised – even in some nationalist
circles – for this casual abandonment of principle. Newspaper
columnists accused Nicola Sturgeon of 'shameless hypocrisy'.[151]
But if the first responsibility of any opposition is to make its
presence felt, the Nationalists were certainly doing that. The
UK government insisted that it had not abandoned its plans to
legalise fox hunting and had merely a delayed them until the
introduction of English Votes for English Laws. But here again
the SNP were able to claim at least a partial victory.

THE BANALITY OF EVEL

In July 2015, David Cameron had planned to push through
– on a standing order motion rather than a full-scale bill – the
controversial measure to exclude Scottish MPs from certain
Commons votes. English Votes for English Laws (EVEL) would
give English MPs an effective veto on legislation 'certified' by
the Speaker as of English only concern. Fox hunting would
clearly be one of such bills. Under EVEL, there would in effect
be an English Grand Committee set up, composed exclusively
of English (and on some occasions Welsh) MPs, which would
have to give its endorsement to any and every Commons bill,
or part thereof, on matters which were already devolved to
Scotland. They would also have a veto on spending motions
and secondary legislation relating exclusively to England.
This would, according to the Prime Minister, address the
anomalies of the West Lothian Question. However, a new raft
of anomalies followed in its train.

The SNP MPs argued that English Votes for English
Laws would make Scottish MPs 'second class citizens' in
the UK parliament and would breach promises made by the
Smith Commission. As explained in previous chapters of this
book, the Nationalists claimed that many nominally 'English'
bills such as those relating to the National Health Service had
an impact on Scotland through the Barnett Formula. But it
wasn't just the SNP who opposed EVEL. The former Scottish
Secretary, the Liberal Democrat MP Alistair Carmichael,
vigorously opposed the measure as 'risky and irresponsible'.
He said the UK government was 'trying to use the United
Kingdom Parliament as a proxy for an English Parliament'.[152]
MPs across the house were concerned that a change of this
magnitude should be properly debated in primary legislation.
Some prominent unionist economists, including Professor Jim
Gallagher of the Constitution Unit, entered the debate over the

summer. He condemned the proposal to allow English MPs to set an exclusively English rate of taxation as incompatible with the union.[153]

In the end, it was a move by the eight Democratic Ulster Unionist MPs that delivered us from EVEL, at least for the time being. They were worried about the impact that English votes might have on the integrity of the United Kingdom, and therefore the security of their province within it. They joined forces with Tory sceptics and forced the government to back down for fear of losing the standing order vote. On July 9th the Conservative Leader of the House, Chris Grayling, announced that he was postponing the measure and would draft revised proposals in the autumn.[154]

The government put a brave face on this setback, but it was undoubtedly a humiliation. The SNP had demonstrated just how fragile David Cameron's majority really was in parliament. What had been intended to demonstrate the impotence of the SNP contingent in Westminster to Scottish voters had done precisely the reverse: it had shown weakness and confusion on the part of the UK government. EVEL has now attracted critical attention in the House of Lords from figures like the former Conservative Scottish Secretary Lord Forsyth.[155] The conundrum of disaggregating the unitary Westminster parliament into regional legislative entities had defeated Gladstone and Lloyd George over a century ago. It was foolhardy of the government to believe that such a profound change could be rushed through on a mere procedural motion.

LORD SEWEL AND THE DEFENCE OF HUMAN RIGHTS

The former SNP leader Alex Salmond was not shy in declaring that the SNP MPs had the UK government on the ropes. They had also – he claimed – been forced to back down over proposals to hold the referendum on membership on the European Union on the same date as the Scottish Parliamentary elections.[156] He also claimed credit for his party in delaying the implementation of the government's plans to abolish the Human Rights Act. This had been heavily trailed by the Conservatives before the general election, but was absent from the 2015 Queen's Speech. The SNP argued that the UK government had no right to abolish the Human Rights Act in Scotland because the European Convention on Human Rights is written into the Scotland Act.

The constitutional position of the Human Rights Act in Scotland is ambiguous. Under the Scotland Act 1998, all acts of the Scottish Parliament must be in compliance with the 1950 European Convention on Human Rights, which affirms citizens' rights to privacy, marriage, freedom of speech etc. But the Human Rights Act, passed by Labour in 2000, is not specifically mentioned in the Scotland Act. Some constitutional theories consequently argued that the Scottish Parliament would be in no position to prevent Westminster repealing the Human Rights Act.[157] The constitution is of course reserved to Westminster. However, the Scottish Government argued that abolition of the Human Rights Act, which permits actions under the ECHR to be mounted in UK courts, would adversely affect citizens' access to human rights in Scotland. Consequently, they asserted that under the Sewel Convention, Westminster would have to seek the consent of the Scottish Parliament before it could abolish the Human Rights Act in the UK, even though it was a UK Act.[158]

The Sewel convention is named after Lord Sewel, the Labour government minister responsible for devolution in the late 1990s. Coincidentally, the peer resigned on 28th July after being filmed allegedly taking drugs while consorting with prostitutes – but his name lives on. The Sewel Convention is not a part of the Scotland Act 1998 either, and it appears only in the 1999 Memorandum of Understanding that accompanied the devolution legislation. But Sewel was supposedly being made a 'permanent' feature of UK constitutional practice by the 2015 Scotland Bill, and there is a studied vagueness about what this permanence actually means.

Nothing in the original Scotland Act or in the 2015 Scotland Bill prevents the UK parliament from legislating on matters devolved to Holyrood: 'The UK parliament remains sovereign in all cases'. But the accepted practice is that there should be a legislative consent motion on any legislation that strays into the responsibilities of the Scottish Parliament. There was a great deal of complex disputation among legal eagles on the Internet over the status of Sewel and the Human Rights Act. But it is certainly arguable that a Sewel motion would be expected if the government pressed ahead with abolishing the Human Rights Act in England. The Scottish Government made it clear that, if David Cameron had pressed ahead with the abolition of the Human Rights Act, there would be a constitutional crisis because the Scottish Parliament under SNP majority control would vote against it.

It's not entirely clear whether the constitutional situation in Scotland was the reason why the UK government postponed the abolition of the Human Rights Act. There were also serious concerns on the Conservative benches about watering down human rights in the UK – or at least appearing to do so. The Tory former Attorney General Dominic Grieve said that abolishing the Human Rights Act would undermine human rights across Europe.[159] One anonymous Conservative minister reportedly threatened to resign. But this didn't stop the SNP claiming victory. Once again they were able to say that, despite their numerical inferiority, they had exposed the weakness of David Cameron's mandate. They certainly alerted the House of Lords to the constitutional implications of abolishing the Human Rights Act, and served notice that Cameron would have a fight on his hands if he persevered.

THE REAL OPPOSITION?

The 56 SNP MPs left Westminster for their first summer recess with their heads held high. They had acted with imagination and discipline, if not always with principle, and had shown that they were not merely a rabble of nationalist troublemakers. The Speaker, John Bercow, even praised them for being "very good parliamentarians".[160]

However, their claim to be the 'real' opposition in Westminster was somewhat inflated. They had succeeded in delaying legislation – not actually defeating it – and the Conservatives had not given up on their plans for English Votes for English Laws. Indeed, David Cameron said that the actions of the SNP on fox hunting made EVEL even more necessary. Certainly, if the press was any guide, English public opinion seemed to resolve to exclude Scottish MPs from English affairs at the earliest opportunity, whatever the constitutional anomalies.

By their presentational success the SNP had also raised expectations that could never really be fulfilled, unless there was a significant change of heart on behalf of Labour about parliamentary cooperation. And this would be a mixed blessing for the Nationalists since their main claim to fame was that they were filling the space – sometimes literally – vacated by a pusillanimous and right wing Labour Party. Alex Salmond was certainly having a new lease of life back in the Westminster parliament he has always found more congenial that Holyrood. But he was not the leader of the SNP, or even the SNP group in Westminster. The real battles were taking place back in Scotland where, in the run up to the 2016 Scottish Parliamentary elections, the SNP leader Nicola Sturgeon was finding herself facing challenges from the left for the first time.

Nicola Sturgeon's popularity continued to soar in the months after the tsunami. According to polls in July and

August, the SNP were now supported by over 60% of voters in Scotland and stood to win nearly all of Labour's constituency seats in the forthcoming Holyrood elections.[161] This was despite growing concern among the same sample of voters about the Scottish government's performance on key issues like education and the economy. The Nicola magic was still working, but her government was starting to creak and hostile critics were beginning to circle.

She was criticised for giving unqualified support to the head of Police Scotland Sir Stephen House, before his surprise resignation in August over issues such the overuse of stop and search powers. Hospital waiting time targets were being breached and there were claims that the SNP had failed to address inequalities in education: children from wealthy homes are twice as likely to leave school with qualifications than children from the poorest.[162] Some prominent Yes supporters like the writer Gerry Hassan became uncharacteristically vocal in their condemnation of the Scottish government's complacency. Hassan said that Nicola Sturgeon's claim to be a true social democrat was 'a sham'. 'The SNP have done precisely nothing to redistribute wealth despite being in government for nearly eight years', he tweeted.

Groups on the left of the SNP such as the Scottish Green Party began refashioning their rhetoric to distance themselves from the SNP in preparation for the 2016 Holyrood elections. The Radical Independence Campaign, which had campaigned so vigorously for a Yes vote during the independence referendum, re-launched itself (minus the Green Party) on 29th August as a new party (or alliance) called RISE. The acronym stands for Respect, Independence, Socialism, Environmentalism.

As explained previously, this Scotdemos as it was nicknamed was modelled on the populist left parties, Podemos in Spain, and Syriza in Greece. Its leading figures, like the trades unionist Cat Boyd, claimed the SNP had shown itself to be a 'centrist party' by its equivocation on issues like fracking and wealth taxes. The RISE star also objected to Nicola Sturgeon's apparent unwillingness to call an early repeat referendum. Boyd echoed the words of the former SNP deputy leader Jim Sillars, who had recently called for an early referendum: 'Our movement is now strong enough to win. The longer we leave it, the more it might ebb away'.[163] There were claims that the failure to schedule a debate on the timing of the next independence referendum during the SNP annual conference in 2015 was a sign the party was losing its radical edge.[164] Suddenly Nicola Sturgeon was being attacked, not only for lacking urgency on social issues, but for lacking urgency on independence.

However, the most immediate challenge to the Sturgeon ascendancy was arguably not from the nationalist far left but from the unionist inside left in the shape of Jeremy Corbyn. Clearly, if the UK Labour Party was capable of electing a left-winger as its leader, whose agenda matched that of the SNP, it was hard for the Nationalists to claim that they were the sole inheritors of social democracy. When Labour's leadership campaign opened in June 2015, no one had believed that the MP for Islington had the remotest chance of becoming Labour leader – not even Corbyn himself. He was the rank outsider and was only nominated to stand at the very last minute by Labour MPs like Margaret Beckett who said they wanted 'a proper debate'. She later said she had been 'a moron' to do so. But the presence of 56 radical left wing SNP MPs in Westminster, defying the Tory government's austerity agenda, seems to have boosted Corbyn's appeal.

Labour experienced something akin to a nervous breakdown after the July Welfare Reform Bill vote debacle, when its Westminster MPs refused to join the SNP in the division lobbies. Many ordinary Labour members were appalled by the apparent capitulation to the Conservative's agenda by the Labour interim leader Harriet Harman (Ed Miliband resigned immediately after Labour's crushing defeat). Almost immediately, support for the left wing candidate, Jeremy Corbyn, in the Labour leadership contest began to mount. Thousands of disillusioned Labour activists and supporters started turning up to Jeremy Corbyn's revivalist meetings, and at one packed event on August 3rd in Camden, Corbyn had to mount a fire engine to address the overspill crowds in the street outside.

Corbyn went on to address overspill crowds at meetings in Scotland later that month. 1500 people turned up to hear him in Glasgow's Old Fruitmarket on 14th August and as many more couldn't get tickets. These were the kind of crowds that had been turning up to hear Nicola Sturgeon over the previous twelve months. The Corbyn bandwagon all but eclipsed the contest for Labour's Scottish leadership, then taking place between the Scottish deputy leader Kezia Dugdale and the former finance spokesman Ken Macintosh.

In a matter of weeks, more than a quarter of a million, mostly younger people, had signed up to Labour as members, or under its £3 supporters scheme. The intention had been to bring in new blood, but this wasn't quite the blood type that the Labour establishment had been looking for. There was some evidence that a few thousand far left, Green Party, SNP, and even Tories also signed up as supporters under a false flag. But what no one denied was that it was Corbyn – with his policies on issues like wealth taxes, rail nationalisation, and nuclear disarmament – had inspired Labour's authentic membership surge.

As I explained earlier, there were striking similarities between the policies of Corbyn and the anti-austerity agenda of the SNP in their 2015 General Election manifesto. Indeed, across the range of issues like the mansion tax, tuition fees, the benefits cap, Keynesian economic policies, gender equality, and immigration, it was hard to discern any significant difference – independence aside – between Corbynism and

Nicola Sturgeon's version of 'utilitarian' civic nationalism. Therefore a Corbyn-led Labour party could at least, in theory, pose a challenge to the social democratic credentials of Nicola Sturgeon and could make it harder for the SNP to attract disillusioned Scottish Labour voters into its fold.

However, it was not yet clear how the Scottish Labour Party would respond to the Corybn tide sweeping through the UK Labour Party. The new Scottish Labour leader Kezia Dugdale initially disowned Corbyn on the grounds that he was too left wing. She said she didn't want Labour to be 'left carping on the sidelines'.[165] However, when she finally met him the day before she herself was declared Labour's Scottish leader, she said he was 'a very nice man'.

Dugdale also announced that she was going to re-open the debate in her party over the renewal of Trident and promised that, in future, the Scottish Labour Party annual conference was going to become a truly democratic forum in which policies proposed by local parties would be debated and voted on. This would appear to open the way for the Scottish party to become more radical by developing its own policies. The Corbyn phenomenon also loosened the grip of the UK Labour establishment on the Scottish Labour Party – if only because they had other things on their mind. As for Jeremy Corbyn himself, there was no indication that he would continue the previous over-centralised approach to the 'branch office' in Scotland. He would almost certainly favour a looser association – the better to allow the Scottish party to combat the SNP. Dugdale has rejected the idea of creating an independent Labour party but, ironically, she may end up having independence thrust upon her.

Corbyn went to considerable lengths not to mention the SNP or even the constitutional debate about independence during his visits to Scotland in August 2015. However, there has never been any doubt about his unionism. He hinted that he would not be averse to electoral arrangements with the SNP after a general election, but he has never supported independence. He believes another referendum is 'neither necessary nor advisable' and he is on record as opposing further powers for the Scottish Parliament. For this reason, the threat to Nicola Sturgeon's dominance of Scottish politics from a revived Labour party looks more theoretical than real.

Labour in Scotland has a new fresh face, but by seeking to draw voters back to Labour from the SNP, Kezia Dugdale has an immense task before her. Sturgeon is sincere about her commitment to social democracy, and while many may argue that she has failed to deliver much in practice, her advocacy remains immensely popular with Scottish voters. Moreover, in her contest with any new Corbyn Labour Party, her party will always have the monopoly of the Scottish dimension. To paraphrase: the SNP may lose some of its utilitarian nationalists to Corbyn, but it will retain its existential ones. Scotland's political marketplace is becoming increasingly crowded with RISE, the Green Party, and possibly a Corbyn-inspired Labour Party vying for votes on the Left. But there is still only one Scottish National Party.

PRECARIATS OF THE WORLD UNITE

The post-referendum political kaleidoscope continues to rearrange itself in novel and unpredictable ways. We are some way from seeing the final picture, but there can be no doubt that we are living through the most exciting and transformative period in Scottish history. In the referendum campaign and the tsunami election we have seen not just a structural change in voter allegiance – not just the emergence of a new and positive sense of Scottish identity – but emergence of a new kind of grass-roots politics. Throughout Scotland people have been turning up to meetings and engaging in political debate in a manner unseen for thirty years. We are seeing unprecedented levels of voter engagement, surges in party memberships, and epic shifts in voting patterns that are simply off the scale of normal democratic politics. This involves all the social classes, but in particular it includes those groups that have been alienated from the political process for decades. This transformation is being led – or a better word might be 'curated' – by a generation of politically engaged citizens who are radicalised by the banking crisis and austerity, connected by social media, and liberated from the archaic political designations of the past. They are predominantly young, working class, and educated.

Much has been written about the global impact of the new forms of collective engagement afforded by social media. The Spanish sociologist Manuel Castells has been tracing the interaction between Internet use, counterculture, and urban protests in books like *Networks of Outrage and Hope* (2015). In the UK, the journalist Paul Mason has popularised some of these ideas in books including *Why It's Kicking Off Everywhere* (2013). He argues that there is something akin to a global uprising – from Egypt to the USA, Iceland to Barcelona – led by a young highly educated but underemployed 'precariat' empowered by social media.

Scotland is not the Middle East or Iceland, but it has a very populous precariat. More than 50% of school leavers go on to higher education here and more than 97,000 students successfully complete higher education courses in Scotland every year.[166] These graduates are pouring into an employment market that is unable to absorb them. Meanwhile, broadband penetration is almost complete in the lowland areas where most Scots live (rural and highland areas are another matter). The decline in the influence of the conventional 'top down' print media has been dramatic in Scotland – a country that used to have the highest newspaper readership in the world – with one third of Scots no longer reading a daily newspaper.[167]

Newspapers like *The Scotsman* have seen their circulations collapse to near insignificance, while online websites like *Wings Over Scotland* now have massive reach. One reason why the pro-union press (and it is overwhelmingly unionist) was so unsuccessful in persuading Scots of the dangers of voting SNP is that far fewer people are reading it than ever before.[168] Nor is the BBC followed with the same loyalty and regard as in other parts of the UK. According to the BBC Trust's own figures, only 48% of Scots believe it adequately reflects their lives in news and current affairs.[169] The BBC has always tended to be seen by Scottish viewers as an institution defined by metropolitan attitudes, while the 'opt out' culture of BBC Scotland is widely resented for being second rate and tokenistic. During the referendum, large numbers of Scottish voters simply stopped believing anything they heard or read in the conventional media.

As it emerged from the 2008-12 economic crisis, Scotland was therefore fertile ground for the spread of new networked social movements. The influence of what is called the 'mainstream media' has largely been broken; the older industrial politics of the Left has largely become moribund. In the thirty years since the defeat of the miners, trades union membership has dwindled outside the public sector and the Labour Party has lost almost all of its mass membership as well as its MPs. To many Scots, Labour seemed like a remote middle-class party defined by the preoccupations of a UK leadership in London. It held little appeal to the radicalised young and working-class Scots who were excited by the idea of making 'a better nation'.

It has generally been assumed that the coming of these networked social movements accelerates the decline of conventional political parties and parliamentary democracy, as such because it is regarded as being under the control of the elites. This is why the new politics is often referred to as 'anti-politics'. But what appears to be happening now, at least in Scotland, is that far from destroying political parties and parliamentary democracy, the Internet age is breathing new life into them. The SNP's membership now stands at 110,000 – more than four times its figure before the referendum campaign – and recently the UK Labour Party has undergone a similar membership explosion.

Turbocharged by the Internet, the 2014 independence referendum campaign brought the largest voter registration in history – 97% – while the referendum itself saw the biggest turnout in electoral history at 85%. The 2015 General Election turnout at 71% was not as high, but the swing to the SNP of 30% on average was the highest ever recorded. This was democratic politics reloaded and energised as we have never seen before. The manner in which support for the SNP spread across Scotland in May 2015, through East and West, highlands and lowlands, working class estates and landed estates, was unprecedented. It was a new kind of almost viral politics, obliterating voting patterns overnight that had endured for a century and more, uniting Scotland geographically as never before behind one national party.

Faced with this turmoil, many commentators simply thought that the Scots 'had gone mad'. Indeed, since the tsunami, the conventional media has tended to downplay the significance of what has happened here, even though the 2015 General Election was the political news event of the century in Scotland. And the explosion in political engagement that began in Scotland has now started to extend UK-wide. The similarity between the independence campaign and the developments in the Labour party following the Corbyn surge are too striking to ignore. People are remaking politics in real time. The most immediate consequence has been the reassertion of Scottish political autonomy, but the reverberations from Scotland's democratic revolution are still being felt. The politics of these islands will never be the same again.

References

1. Andrew Marr's diary: Why this is such a tooth-grindingly awful election, Andrew Marr, *The Spectator*, 11/04/2015, http://bit.ly/1I9uabx

2. Should Labour fear 'Pasokification'? Tim Bale, *Policy Network*, 10/03/2015, http://bit.ly/1dbis2V

3. UK Election Lets 'Scottish Lion' Roar, Jason Douglas, *Wall Street Journal*, 08/05/2015, http://on.wsj.com/1N0CHww

4. David Cameron: Miliband would not be legitimate as PM if Labour came second, Rowena Mason and Frances Perraudin, *The Guardian*, 05/05/2105, http://bit.ly/1ALaGYO

5. John Major warns of 'clear and present SNP danger' – in an incoherent whisper, John Crace, *The Guardian*, 21/04/2015, http://bit.ly/1KJX1Vq

6. *The Daily Mail*, 25/4/15

7. Labour Lost because of Scotland. It's that simple.[Almost], Ed Stradling, Blog, 12/05/2015 http://bit.ly/1THP461; Labour haven't just failed to win – it's worse than that, Paul Mason, Channel 4 Blog, 08/05/2015, http://bit.ly/1AJvNW6

8. The undoing of Ed Miliband – and how Labour lost the election, Patrick Wintour, *The Guardian*, 11/06/2015, http://bit.ly/1KangD7

9. General Election 2015: Prospect of Labour-SNP coalition makes one in four voters less likely to support Ed Miliband, says survey, Andrew Grice and James Cusick, *The Independent*, 29/04/2015, http://ind.pn/1JNeJ6h

10. How the SNP-Tory dynamics shifted the 2015 election, Martin Shaw, Open Democracy, 05/06/2015, http://bit.ly/1BGN2gS

11. Tories edge ahead and plan to sit tight in No 10, Tim Shipman, Marie Woolf and James Lyons, *The Sunday Times*, 03/05/2015, http://thetim.es/1KIUI1Z

12. Lord O'Donnell: leader of largest party does not automatically become PM, Nicholas Watt, *The Guardian*, 06/05/2015, http://bit.ly/1GVGF9T

13. Why the Scottish nationalists cannot call the shots, Phillip Stephens, *The Financial Times*, 21/04.2015, http://on.ft.com/1QM3H9w

14. Cameron's campaign is "poisonous" for Scots Tories, says party's former press chief, Magnus Gardham, *The Herald*, 29/04/2015, http://bit.ly/1FSbDxG

15. As the Tories struggle to defeat Miliband, they are hoping others will do the job for them, George Eaton, *The New Statesmen*, 08/04/2015, http://bit.ly/1HRVM1H

16. Ed Balls: Labour will eliminate budget deficit by 2020, Nicholas Watt, *The Guardian*, 13/04/2015, http://bit.ly/1ALbWeq

17. Jim Murphy hits out at SNP's 'austerity max', (un-attributed), *The Scotsman*, 13/04/2015, http://bit.ly/1JhtD8k

18. Full fiscal autonomy delayed? The SNP's plans for further devolution to Scotland, David Phillips, Institute For Fiscal Studies, 21/04/2015, http://bit.ly/1K1Ccla

19. Ed Balls to reject SNP's £180bn spending demand, David Maddox, *The Scotsman*, 26/02/2015, http://bit.ly/1eN6CNX

20. Nicola Sturgeon attacks 'Westminster austerity economics', (un-attributed), BBC News, 11/02/2015, http://bbc.in/1AkyMHG

21. Scotland's black hole under SNP's fiscal autonomy plan would balloon to almost £10bn by 2020, says IFS, Michael Settle, *The Herald*, 22/04/2015, http://bit.ly/1HTSNba

22. Tories have £30bn black hole in spending plans, says IFS, Heather Stewart, *The Guardian*, 23/04/2015, http://bit.ly/1aUzv8h

23. Reality Check: Why should we trust the IFS?, Sebastian Chrispin, 23/04/2015, http://bbc.in/1BH4ooi

24. Sturgeon and Balls dismiss IFS analysis as 'wrong', Josh May, 23/04/2015, http://bit.ly/1BH4vAj

25. Sturgeon booed as she hints at ANOTHER independence referendum: SNP leader uses Scottish TV debate to say she can make Miliband PM and will NEVER prop up a Cameron government, Daniel Martin, *The Daily Mail*, 07/04/2015, http://dailym.ai/1K6WawO

26. Labour trust falls after Better Together Tory pact, Andrew Whitaker, *The Scotsman*, 26/01/2015, http://bit.ly/1I8QXlH

27. Last-minute tactical voting could decide the election, George Parker and Jim Pickard, *The Financial Times*, 06/05/2015, http://on.ft.com/1K72yW5

28. Scotland has gone mad, Chris Deerin, CapX, 07/04/2015, http://bit.ly/1PgayVi

29. Scottish referendum: shared values matter more than where the border lies, Polly Toynbee, *The Guardian*, 19/08/2014, http://bit.ly/1ftlHo6

30. How Scotland Lost Its Mind, Iain Martin, Standpoint, 05/2015, http://bit.ly/1H6VXZa

31. Election 2015: David Blunkett warns of SNP 'tsunami', (un-attributed), BBC News, 30/04/2015, http://bbc.in/1HVtAgm

32. Alex Salmond: I joked about writing Labour Budget, (un-attributed), BBC News, 22/04/2015, http://bbc.in/1FpuyfI

33. Hedge fund boss gives Conservatives their biggest donation in six years, Rowena Mason, *The Guardian*, 15/05/2015, http://bit.ly/1RH9nyr

34. SNP conspicuously absent from list of new political donations, Jim Pickard, *The Financial Times*, 23/04/2015, http://on.ft.com/1Lg4dbb

35. Labour man Ian Smart: New SNP MPs Trots and fascists, Staff Writer, *The National*, 13/05/2015, http://bit.ly/1Bx0hAc

36. Record numbers of female and minority-ethnic MPs in new House of Commons, Helena Bengtsson, Sally Weale

and Libby Brooks, *The Guardian*, 08/05/2015, http://bit.
ly/1ALjzMJ

37. Half of new cabinet was privately educated, Sutton Trust
(Press Release), 11/05/2015, http://bit.ly/1I7WifS

38. What Are The New SNP Candidates Like?, John
McDermott, *The Financial Times*, 22/04/2015, http://on.ft.
com/1Nfwaz1

39. 'SNP are Marxists', says Conservative MP, Doug Bolton,
The Independent, 10/05/2015, http://ind.pn/1E0NEry

40. Gordon Wilson: pro-indy campaigners are arguing
'with all excitement of robot', (un-attributed), *The Herald*,
13/08/2013, http://bit.ly/1dc3LNB

41. Sir Gerald Kaufman calls SNP MPs 'goons' over their
Commons behaviour, Frances Perraudin, *The Guardian*,
21/05/2015, http://bit.ly/1FpvtNp

42. Fury as MP calls Scots leader 'wee lass in tin helmet':
Labour whip given a dressing down by party after
'disgraceful slur', John Stevens, *The Daily Mail*, 08/03/2015,
http://dailym.ai/1AUDTto

43. Boris Johnson sparks fury after claiming SNP in
government is like getting 'King Herod to run a baby farm',
Andrew Woodcock, *The Daily Record*, 20/05/2015, http://bit.
ly/1Q3iqwr

44. SNP deal with Labour would be match made in hell, says
David Cameron, Rowena Mason and Robert Booth, *The
Guardian*, 20/04/2015, http://bit.ly/1J3Kj30

45. Nicola Sturgeon insults: the worst attacks directed at the SNP leader, Jessica Elgot, *The Guardian*, 21/04/2015, http://bit.ly/1RHcciX

46. Rise of Nicola Sturgeon: from 'nippy sweetie' to SNP leader?, (un-attributed), Channel 4 Blog, 24/09/2014, http://bit.ly/1tZktoa

47. It's the Esh-NP! Nicola Sturgeon tells the Loose Women she had voice coaching from Sean Connery, Tom McTague, MailOnline, 11/05/2015, http://dailym.ai/1GCGkr3

48. The triumph of Nicola Sturgeon, Ian Jack, *The Guardian*, 23/04/2015, http://bit.ly/1Eudtr1

49. Nicola Sturgeon's Biography, Rosemary Goring, *The Herlad*, 28/03/2015, http://bit.ly/1M0VUOg

50. Scottish deputy first minister apologises over fraudster letter, Severin Carrell, *The Guardian*, 24/02/2010, http://bit.ly/1LgeWSU

51. Did Nicola Sturgeon Hack The Hair From Her Sister's Barbie Doll?, Oliver Harvey, Sun Nation, 25/04/2015, http://bit.ly/1Nfxn9u

52. *Nicola Sturgeon: A Political Life*, David Torrance, (Birlinn, 2015), http://bit.ly/1FwNzN2

53. New First Minister Nicola Sturgeon hopes her success will inspire women, Paul Gilbride, The Express, 20/11/2014, http://bit.ly/1FpEqGo

54. Alex: I want Jack's job, (un-attributed), *Linlithgow Gazette*, 28/07/2004, http://bit.ly/1FrJzPl

55. How can we curb the authoritarian drift of Scotland?, Walter Humes, *Scottish Review* (undated), http://bit.ly/1LwkqH6

56. SNP postpones FFA push in battle for 'Smith plus', (unattributed), *The Scotsman*, 31/05/2015, http://bit.ly/1d6XqCV

57. Under-fire police chief in the dock over stop and search row, Daniel Sanderson, *The Herald*, 20/02/2015, http://bit.ly/1eE5AE8

58. Welcome to Scotland, the SNP's police state, Kevin McKenna, *The Guardian*, 19/01/2014, http://bit.ly/1dNA0hR

59. Nicola Sturgeon denies saying she wanted David Cameron to win election, Severin Carrell and Nicholas Watt, *The Guardian*, 03/04/2015, http://bit.ly/1FadOcP

60. Carmichael faces court over leaked Sturgeon memo, Scott MacNab, *The Scotsman*, 30/05/2015, http://bit.ly/1TKB7Eu

61. It's an insult say families as SNP chief Nicola Sturgeon snubs Afghanistan war memorial service, Larisa Brown and Alan Roden and Harriet Crawford, *The Daily Mail*, 14/03/2015, http://dailym.ai/1fwuB4t

62. *The Guardian*, 21/4/15

63. Nicola Sturgeon hailed 'Queen of Scotland' after 'hammering Westminster's old boys network' in TV triumph, Tom McTague, MailOnline, http://dailym.ai/1BHkqON

64. Poll shows Sturgeon is now the most popular politician across Britain, Michael Settle, *The Herald*, 29/04/2015, http://bit.ly/1Im8uZ8

65. Scotland could hold a second referendum without David Cameron's approval, suggests senior SNP source, Matt Dathan, *The Independent*, 15/05/2015, http://ind.pn/1Hb1rC8

66. Gordon Wilson: SNP has sidelined independence in favour of federalism, Magnus Gardham, *The Herald*, 02/06/2015, http://bit.ly/1BysFC8

67. Jim Murphy Blames Union Boss As He Resigns As Scottish Labour Leader, Alain Tolhurst, SunNation, 16/05/2015, http://bit.ly/1IbQr8u

68. Splits begin to emerge over autonomous Scottish Labour party suggestions, Liam O'Hare, Common Space, 18/05/2015, http://bit.ly/1LySPVy

69. Nicola Sturgeon talks up minority government while waving goodbye to the Tories, Hilary Duncanson, *The Daily Record*, 06/05/2015, http://bit.ly/1FLblFB

70. From station to Subway - the flight of Iain Gray, (un-attributed), *The Scotsman*, 07/04/2011, http://bit.ly/1CqwOmP

71. Johann Lamont resigns: Party has 'no clue' on Scotland, says former Labour first minister, Jane Merrick, *The Independent*, 26/10/2014, http://ind.pn/1SG6Hlc

72. Labour leader Johann Lamont demands end to 'something for nothing' culture, (un-attributed), STV, 25/09/2012, http://bit.ly/JgIsuO

73. Scottish NHS becomes key issue in independence as doctors debate future, Denis Campbell, *The Guardian*, 15/09/2014, http://bit.ly/1nZE8P4

74. I won't let an independent Scotland keep the pound, says Ed Miliband, Severin Carrell, *The Guardian*, 08/08/2014, http://bit.ly/1svQjWQ

75. All things to all men, Rev. Stuart Campbell, Wings Over Scotland, 25/11/2014, http://bit.ly/1ddMfIv

76. Free school meals for primary one to three pupils in Scotland, (un-attributed), BBC News, 05/01/2015, http://bbc.in/1AvicUY

77. Jim Murphy to call for 'devo max within Scotland', Jane Bradley, *The Scotsman*, 05/12/2014, http://bit.ly/1RsTMjX

78. Jim Murphy unveils plan to rewrite Scottish Labour's Clause IV, George Eaton, *The New Statesman*, 15/12/2014, http://bit.ly/1yRAhNp

79. I have never been a Unionist: Murphy, Magnus Gardham, *The Herald*, 14/01/2015, http://bit.ly/1LiUkti

80. Jim Murphy hits out at SNP's 'austerity max', (un-attributed), *The Scotsman*, 13/04/2015, http://bit.ly/1JhtD8k

81. Scottish Labour's New Policy: Vote Tory, Rev. Stuart Campbell, Wings Over Scotland, 23/02/2015, http://bit.ly/1K9zPzH

82. TV debate: It's a rammy at the BBC, Daniel Sanderson, *The Herald*, 13/04/2015, http://bit.ly/1TKP7Oz

83. *The Independent*, 13/4/15

84. Scots see England as a 'piggy bank', says Shropshire MP Owen Paterson, (un-attributed), *Shropshire Star*, 15/05/2015, http://bit.ly/1K8d6m1

85. 'Bored' Tom Harris posts dog re-election video, (un-attributed), *The Scotsman*, 04/05/2015, http://bit.ly/1ddPbVx

86. Labour insiders: saving Curran's a drain on resources, Paul Hutcheson, *The Herald*, 08/03/2015, http://bit.ly/18sdlsS

87. Jim Murphy Blames Union Boss As He Resigns As Scottish Labour Leader, Alain Tolhurst, SunNation, 16/05/2015, http://bit.ly/1IbQr8u

88. Labour in Scotland will 'die like dinosaurs' unless they change, warns former MSP, Kathleen Nutt, *The National*, 10/06/2015, http://bit.ly/1eFH59O

89. Andy Burnham pushes Labour to set up separate pro-European Union campaign, Patrick Wintour, *The Guardian*, 02/06/2015, http://bit.ly/1BKuNRZ

90. General Election 2015: Son of former Labour leader Neil Kinnock wins in Aberavon, Alicia Melville-Smith, Wales Online, 8/05/2015, http://bit.ly/1N4VgzU

91. The women who refused to lie for Tommy Sheridan, Julie Bindel, *The Guardian*, 28/01/2011, http://bit.ly/1Hbo37o

92. The women who refused to lie for Tommy Sheridan, Julie Bindel, *The Guardian*, 28/01/2011, http://bit.ly/1Hbo37o

93. Andy Coulson cleared of perjury as Scottish court case collapses, Severin Carrell and Lisa O'Carroll, 03/05/2015, http://bit.ly/1N4Y4gp

94. Hope Over Fear?, Robin McAlpine, Bella Caledonia, 28/04/2015, http://bit.ly/1FumWgQ

95. Loki vs National Collective: A timeline of the debate over democracy and artistic dissent, Angela Haggerty, Common Space, 12/03/2015, http://bit.ly/1Ap8gbv

96. Alex Massie: Where's the art, National Collective?, Alex Massie, *The Scotsman*, 14/03/2015, http://bit.ly/1GuqEsW

97. Alex Massie: Where's the art, National Collective?, Alex Massie, *The Scotsman*, 14/03/2015, http://bit.ly/1GuqEsW

98. Record View: Wings Over Scotland website fuels hatred and paranoia, (un-attributed, *The Daily Record*, 25/02/2015, http://bit.ly/1ddSBHJ

99. Weekly Wanker #017: Wings Over Scotland, Tarzan Girl, A Thousand Flowers, 01/09/2009, http://bit.ly/1g6IEdy

100. Yes Together: Robin McAlpine, Wings Over Scotland, and the progressive whitewashing of misogyny, @pastachips, Better Nation, 24/06/2014, http://bit.ly/1HWcRGb

101. Debate, feminist-style, Rev. Stuart Campbell, Wings Over Sealand, http://bit.ly/1F3TSHC

102. WingsScotland_transphobia, (un-attributed), Edinburgh Eye, 13/06/2014, http://bit.ly/1Kk9wFR

103. Ugly witches are easy to hunt, Rev. Stuart Campbell, Wings Over Scotland, 04/03/2012, http://bit.ly/1T6N1Im

104. Greens walk out on the Yes campaign, Tom Gordon, *The Herald*, 10/06/2012, http://bit.ly/1KkaFNH

105. Stewart Hosie calls for Yes Alliance, Mike Small, Bella Caledonia, 21/10/2014, http://bit.ly/1wmDBvf

106. Why Scotland needs a pop up constitutional convention., Iain Macwhirter, Iain Macwhiter (Blog), 17/10/2014, http://bit.ly/1dq7JlD

107. Common Weal criticised for unpaid workers ad, Tom Peterkin, *The Scotsman*, 04/11/2014, http://bit.ly/1HhZ2pR

108. Socialists' Liam to pay a visit to Cumbernauld, (un-attributed), *Cumbernauld News*, 28/03/2015, http://bit.ly/1TLaKOD

109. Left Project Welcomes SSP Support For A New Left Electoral Alliance, (un-attributed), Left Project, 25/05/2015, http://bit.ly/1K9RveL

110. Jon Cruddas: this could be the greatest crisis the Labour party has ever faced, Toby Helm, *The Observer*, 16/05/2015, http://bit.ly/1JQMuUT

111. Peter Jones: Ireland's exit a lesson for Cameron, Peter Jones, *The Scotsman*, 11/05/2015, http://bit.ly/1JyOQLk

112. David Cameron says no to second Scottish referendum - as it happened, Michael Wilkinson, *The Telegraph*, 15/05/2015, http://bit.ly/1JMCko5

113. Scottish independence would weaken UK's global status, says ex-Nato chief, Severin Carrell, *The Guardian*, 08/04/2014, http://bit.ly/1mYzd1d

114. Scottish independence would weaken UK's global status, says ex-Nato chief, Severin Carrell, *The Guardian*,

08/04/2014, http://bit.ly/1mYzd1d

115. Scotland has gone mad, Chris Deerin, CapX, 07/04/2015, http://bit.ly/1PgayVi

116. David Cameron says he could give Scotland more powers after meeting with Nicola Sturgeon, Katrine Bussey and Jon Stone, *The Independent*, 15/05/2015, http://ind.pn/1IwD1jj

117. Nicola Sturgeon talks up minority government while waving goodbye to the Tories, Hilary Duncanson, *The Daily Record*, 06/05/2015, http://bit.ly/1FLblFB

118. The Calman Commission's recommendations at a glance, Simon Johnson, *The Telegraph*, 15/06/2009, http://bit.ly/1JCUn1S

119. Commission on the Future Governance of Scotland, Lord Strathclyde, Scottish Conservatives, 06/2014, http://bit.ly/1pzN0iV

120. Tom Devine: Scottish independence 'more likely than ever', (un-attributed), BBC News, 24/05/2015, http://bbc.in/1IV2RCH

121. EU Vote 'May Trigger New Scots Referendum', (un-attributed), Sky News, 10/05/2015, http://bit.ly/1IpCl1w

122. Two Different Countries? Scottish and English Attitudes to Equality and Europe, John Curtice, What Scotland Thinks, 18/10/2013, http://bit.ly/1JySPY4

123. Federalism Revisited, Lord Foulkes, Lord Foulkes (Blog), 2012, http://bit.ly/1IpCIcl

124. David Torrance: Why Cameron should see answering Scottish question as an opportunity, David Torrance, *The Herald*, 18/05/2015, http://bit.ly/1ESenYa

125. Cameron sparks anger over English income tax rate, David Maddox, *The Scotsman*, 14/04/2015, http://bit.ly/1dXH4xm

126. Election 2015: Smith Commission a 'shambles', says Jack McConnell, (un-attributed), UK News, 10/05/2015, http://bit.ly/1HirMi7

127. Smith Commission leaves Barnett formula 'increasingly unfit for purpose', Richard Johnstone, PublicFinance, 27/11/2014, http://bit.ly/1Ic6K5i

128. Scotland's black hole under SNP's fiscal autonomy plan would balloon to almost £10bn by 2020, says IFS, Michael Settle, *The Herald*, 22/04/2015, http://bit.ly/1HTSNba

129. *Devolution in the United Kingdom*, Vernon Bogdanor, (Oxford University Press, 1999), http://bit.ly/1FyX52k

130. George Kerevan: Scottish fiscal autonomy is best option for all, George Kerevan, *The National*, 15/06/2015, http://bit.ly/1Ka0pZz

131. Majority of under 60s support Scotland's independence, Richard Wood, HITC Politics, 09/2014, http://bit.ly/1fxhfF2

132. *Independence of the Scottish Mind: Elite Narratives, Public Spaces and the Making of a Modern Nation*, Gerry Hassan, (Palgrave MacMillan, 2014), http://bit.ly/1GERgV0

133. How Sturgeon struck up special relationship in US, David Torrance, *The Scotsman*, 14/06/2015, http://bit.ly/1e1Gdv2

134. Support for independence increases, (un-attributed), *The Southern Reporter*, 24/05/2015, http://bit.ly/1GES10i

135. Independence of the Scottish mind has shown up the failure of British nationalism, Gerry Hassan, *The New Statesman*, 10/09/2014, http://bit.ly/1rGavDs

136. For Scotland, independence day has already dawned, Neal Ascherson, *The Guardian*, 10/05/2015, http://bit.ly/1F1kVa1

137. Statute of Westminster 1931, British Government, 1931, http://bit.ly/1eFRSkk

138 Tory and SNP fail in joint full fiscal autonomy bid, David Maddox, *The Scotsman*, 15/06/2015, http://bit.ly/1N2jVY0

139 House of Commons Scotland Bill, 29/06/2015, http://bit.ly/1KHi22z

140 Westminster is warning Scotland the SNP's plans will leave us broke. They're lying, says Alex Salmond, Alex Salmond, *The National*, 13/04/2015, http://bit.ly/1GZB41s

141 SNP dissatisfied with Cameron's Scottish devolution plans, Muir Dickie, *Financial Times*, 27/05/2015, http://on.ft.com/1EBgW7E

142 "Stop bleating" about Scotland Bill, Mundell's professor tells SNP, Tom Gordon, *The Herald*, 31/05/2015, http://bit.ly/1KHiga0

143 Oral Answers to Questions - The Prime Minister, They Work For You, 01/07/2015, http://bit.ly/1L4m7cV

144 Ruth Davidson condemns income tax rise 'myth', *The Scotsman*, 21/01/2015

145 Diary of a tax advisor: Scotland's new income tax, Economia, 18/05/2015, http://bit.ly/1VvVQf9

146 Mhairi Black is inspiring, wonderful – and utterly wrong, Deborah Orr, *The Guardian*, 18/07/2015, http://bit.ly/1COhh5R

147 Mhairi Black maiden speech in full: SNP MP tears apart Conservative Government and Labour opposition, Kashmira Gander, *The Independent*, 15/07/2015, http://ind.pn/1f3wxRm

148 SNP takes to opposition seats after blasting Labour for welfare bill stance, Nadia Khomami, *The Guardian*, 21/07/2015, http://bit.ly/1L4mkNr

149 Feeble Fifty taunt could come back to haunt the SNP, Torcuil Crichton, *Daily Record*, 30/04/2015, http://bit.ly/1LKJFq7

150 With her cynical foxhunting vote, Sturgeon has joined the Westminster club, Simon Jenkins, *The Guardian*, 14/07/2015, http://bit.ly/1VvVZPz

151 Hypocritical, shameless, unprincipled: Sturgeon's stance on hunting is just the start of her war on England, Chris Deerin, Mail Online, 15/07/2015

152 Carmichael blasts "risky and irresponsible" EVEL plans as Government run away from their own policy, Alistair

Carmichael, 08/07/2015, http://bit.ly/1LW2g4I

153 English votes for English taxes? The EVEL proposals' implications for tax and spending, 10/07/2015, The Constitution Unit, http://bit.ly/1UmqOsX

154 English votes for English laws plan to be revised after Commons revolt, Nicholas Watt, *The Guardian,* 09/07/2015, http://bit.ly/1LKJJGw

155 Evel vote could test Cameron's Commons majority, Kate Devlin, *The Herald,* 02/07/15, http://bit.ly/1IIRisr

156 Government sees off EU referendum rebellion, ITV News, 16/06/2015, http://bit.ly/1JLKbER

157 Scotland, Sewel, and the Human Rights Act, David Scott, Human Rights Blog, 18/07/2015, http://bit.ly/1HRWrBt

158 Sturgeon picks her first fight: SNP leader tells PM he can't scrap Human Rights Act in Scotland, Matt Chorley, Mail Online, 12/05/2015, http://dailym.ai/1Urirad

159 Tory plans will destroy human rights across Europe, warns Dominic Grieve, Owen Bowcott, *The Guardian,* 11/06/2015, http://bit.ly/1L4mQLi

160 Commons Speaker praises work of new SNP MPs at Westminster, The Courier, 14/08/2015, http://bit.ly/1hxO4m3

161 Nicola Sturgeon's bandwagon rolls on: a new poll puts the SNP on 62%, Alan Massie, *The Spectator,* 10/08/2015, http://bit.ly/1JxQkB7

162 Inequality and a reality check for the SNP, David Torrance, *The Herald,* 21/06/2015, http://bit.ly/1XfuueZ

163 Our movement is winning the argument … let's not wait for indyref2, Cat Boyd, *The National,* 11/08/2015, http://bit.ly/1EBfiTw

164 Exclusive: No mention of indyref 1 or 2 in provisional SNP conference agenda, David Jamieson, Common Space, 04/08/2015, http://bit.ly/1MaB3f7

165 Kezia Dugdale: Corbyn win could leave Labour 'carping on sidelines', Libby Brooks, *The Guardian,* 02/08/2015, http://bit.ly/1MGegrC

166 Could Scotland's talented workforce work for your GBS centre?, Scottish Development International, 29/04/2015, http://bit.ly/1JLKsYx

167 'Fewer than half of Scots' are reading a daily newspaper, Doug Kennedy, BBC News, 04/08/2015, http://bbc.in/1JMSg7U

168 *Democracy in the Dark: The Decline of the Scottish Press and How to Keep the Lights On,* Iain Macwhirter, Saltire Society, http://bit.ly/1KHz0hp

169 BBC does not reflect our lives, say half of Scots, Phil Miller, *The Herald,* 17/07/15, http://bit.ly/1VvWycc

All quotes taken from We are the 56 by Josiah Bircham and Grant Costello (Freight, 2015)

Appendix

1. Alex Salmond
Constituency: Gordon
Year of Birth: 1954

Quote: "The 56 are fantastic. [...] In terms of talent, raw political talent, and breadth of ability, this is an extraordinary group and a deep reservoir of skilled politicians."

2015 General Election Result: SNP gain from Liberal Democrats with a 14.9% majority.

2. Chris Law
Constituency: Dundee West
Year of Birth: 1969

Quote: "I think we can continue developing that sense of common weal and knowing that the balance of a good society is opportunity, productivity, and entrepreneurialism, but it should never be at the expense of those less fortunate."

2015 General Election Result: SNP gain from Labour with a 38.2% majority.

3. Stewart Hosie

Constituency: Dundee East

Year of Birth: 1963

Quote: "What I'm finding is that the quality is incredibly high [in Westminster]. It only took a few days at Westminster and the Maiden Speeches to start for some of the rather snide comments about the quality of our new members to be completely put to bed."

2015 General Election Result: SNP hold with a 39.8% majority.

4. Stuart Donaldson

Constituency: West Aberdeenshire and Kincardine

Year of Birth: 1991

Quote: "The people and the communities have made me the person that I am today, so it is really now about helping them. But also about standing up and representing Scotland more widely. We try and fulfil the expectations and the trust that the people of Scotland placed on us, and I remember that every single day."

2015 General Election Result: SNP gain from Liberal Democrats with a 12.7% majority.

5. Mike Weir

Constituency: Angus

Year of Birth: 1958

Quote: "I had the opportunity to go to university because of my fees being paid and a grant. I've also been very grateful to the National Health Service in the course of my life. These are things that are frightfully important to me and are things that should be the bedrock of any society."

2015 General Election Result: SNP hold with a 25.2% majority.

6. Kirsty Blackman
Constituency: Aberdeen North
Year of Birth: 1986

Quote: "[Former SNP MSP] Brian [Adam] is the reason that those of us round here have an ethos for casework. [...] He always said that the most important thing was casework, it was to do your best for people and try and make life better for people. He was so absolutely right."

2015 General Election Result: SNP gain from Labour with a 30.5% majority.

7. Callum McCaig
Constituency: Aberdeen South
Year of Birth: 1985

Quote: "I had always been an SNP supporter, my folks were always supporters, so it just seemed like the natural thing to do was the join the party."

2015 General Election Result: SNP gain from Labour with a 14.9% majority.

8. Eilidh Whiteford

Constituency: Banff and Buchan
Year of Birth: 1969

Quote: "I still look back on it as one of the proudest days of my life, when 250,000 people marched through Edinburgh [for Make Poverty History]. [...] We worked so hard to make it happen and we couldn't believe how many people showed up. But for me I was really proud that Scotland showed up."
2015 General Election Result: SNP hold with a 31.4% majority.

9. Brendan O'Hara

Constituency: Argyll and Bute
Year of Birth: 1963

Quote: "What we have to remember is that we are standing on the shoulders of giants. People have dedicated their lives to this cause in full knowledge that they would never be remembered."

2015 General Election Result: SNP gain from Liberal Democrats with a 16.3% majority.

10. Paul Monaghan

Constituency: Caithness, Sutherland, and Easter Ross
Year of Birth: 1966

Quote: "I come from a family that aren't particularly political, but for as long as I can remember I've always been interested in politics. I've always been interested in the organisation of society and how it's structured and governed."

2015 General Election Result: SNP gain from Liberal Democrats with a 11.2% majority.

11. Drew Hendry
Constituency: Inverness, Nairn, Badenoch and Strathspey
Year of Birth: 1964

Quote: "I am always aware of the old phrase, 'standing on the shoulders of giants'. I know that I wouldn't be here today if it hadn't been for the work of the people during the 1979 campaign and the future campaigns."

2015 General Election Result: SNP gain from Liberal Democrats with a 18.8% majority.

12. Angus Robertson
Constituency: Moray
Year of Birth: 1969

Quote: "I can't wait for Scotland to become independent again, confident, excited about opportunities, focused on the societal and economic challenges we have and [being] the most successful country we can be."

2015 General Election Result: SNP hold with a 18.4% majority

13. Angus Brendan MacNeil
Constituency: Na h-Eileanan an Iar or the Hebrides and Western Isles
Year of Birth: 1970

Quote: "We are ultimately controlled by a government who only has one MP in Scotland: these are the consequences of a No vote in the Referendum, it means these big decisions are out of our hands and the Tories can cut everybody. It's scarier than any scare story you heard before the Referendum."

2015 General Election Result: SNP hold with a 25.7% majority.

14. Ian Blackford
Constituency: Ross, Skye and Lochaber
Year of Birth: 1961

Quote: "I remember going to my next SNP branch meeting in Portree the Monday after the vote and it was a 'wow' moment for me. There was a sense of resolve at that meeting and it took me back. Soon then after a discussion with my wife and many others I decided that running in [the General Election in] 2015 was something that I wanted to do."

2015 General Election Result: SNP gain from Liberal Democrats with a 12.3% majority.

15. Anne McLaughlin
Constituency: Glasgow North East
Year of Birth: 1966

Quote: "In 2007 when Alex Salmond announced he was to be First Minister of Scotland, the other parties could have stopped it. But he did it with such confidence that Labour and the Lib Dems were taken aback. From then on, as a party, we had the opportunity to govern and we proved ourselves."

2015 General Election Result: SNP gain from Labour with a 24.4% majority.

16. Patrick Grady
Constituency: Glasgow North
Year of Birth: 1980

Quote: "I remember being fifteen, and being taken to the Eden Court in Inverness. We were all at the top gallery watching this political speech [by Alex Salmond]."

2015 General Election Result: SNP gain from Labour with a 25.2% majority.

17. Alison Thewliss
Constituency: Glasgow Central
Year of Birth: 1982

Quote: "[At high school] we had speakers from all the political parties that came to the school and the SNP speaker had talked about the idea of building fairer Scotland through independence. I thought there and then that it was the SNP I wanted to get involved in."

2015 General Election Result: SNP gain from Labour with a 27% majority.

18. Stewart McDonald
Constituency: Glasgow South
Year of Birth: 1986

Quote: "Retail staff are incredibly under-paid, over-worked, not valued properly, and are often working in very poor conditions and long hours. When you go through that yourself, and that is your only source of income which is usually the minimum wage, you start to think surely we can treat people better."

2015 General Election Result: SNP gain from Labour with a 25.1% majority.

19. Chris Stephens
Constituency: Glasgow South West
Year of Birth: 1973

Quote: "Pollok had the highest individual number of Yes votes in Glasgow. [...] I thought we were going to win [the Referendum]. Our experience in Pollok and the enthusiasm we saw in the lead up to the vote was inspiring."

2015 General Election Result: SNP gain from Labour with a 24.3% majority.

20. Carol Monaghan
Constituency: Glasgow North West
Year of Birth: Unknown

Quote: "I had always voted for the SNP, but my family had always been Labour-voting. My dad [...] had got himself out of poverty through hard work, and he always instilled the confidence to make your own decisions in his kids."

2015 General Election Result: SNP gain from Labour with a 23.6% majority.

21. Natalie McGarry
Constituency: Glasgow East
Year of Birth: 1981

Quote: "The Labour Party were throwing everything and

the kitchen sink at Glasgow East [during the 2015 General Election]. What that demonstrated was the complete lack of awareness on the Labour Party's part about what people in the constituency were telling them."

2015 General Election Result: SNP gain from Labour with a 24.5% majority.

22. Margaret Ferrier
Constituency: Rutherglen and Hamilton West
Year of Birth: 1961

Quote: "I think at the start I didn't want to believe I was being persuaded [by the SNP] because I was always brought up to be a Labour voter. A lot of what [Alex Salmond] was saying made sense to me. Eventually, as I started to listen more, I found that a lot of it really resonated with me."

2015 General Election Result: SNP gain from Labour with a 17.3% majority.

23. Martin Docherty
Constituency: West Dunbartonshire
Year of Birth: 1971

Quote: "[The SNP] was a party that spoke to me about certain areas of social justice and the idea that government should be as local as possible. In terms of my identity, I never felt an affinity with the UK [...] so my natural inclination was to join the SNP and I did so when I was twenty-one."

2015 General Election Result: SNP gain from Labour with a 27.7% majority.

24. Mhairi Black
Constituency: Paisley and Renfrewshire South
Year of Birth: 1994

Quote: "[After the 2014 Referendum] I thought we had fought too hard for this and I am not going back in my box. What amazed and heartened me was I was not the only person feeling that way – it became very clear very quickly, with the surge in membership of the SNP, that something was changing."

2015 General Election Result: SNP gain from Labour with a 12.3% majority.

25. Gavin Newlands
Constituency: Paisley and Renfrewshire North
Year of Birth: 1980

Quote: "I want to make the lives of my constituents easier. Whether that is through the power of argument, protecting them from Tory cuts, or helping them through the office of being an MP, I want to do whatever it takes to make their lives easier."

2015 General Election Result: SNP gain from Labour with a 18.0% majority.

26. Ronnie Cowan
Constituency: Inverclyde
Year of Birth: Unknown

Quote: "In 1971 we had a mock election in my primary school and I stood for the SNP. I have no idea why or what put me there [...] To be honest when I was eleven years of age it would've been more about flags and sport and the 'we're Scottish' type thing that put me there but I joined the party when I was sixteen."

2015 General Election Result: SNP gain from Labour with a 24.8% majority.

27. Alan Brown
Constituency: Kilmarnock and Loudoun
Year of Birth: 1970

Quote: "Clearly the catalyst for the dramatic change at Westminster has been the Referendum and the negative campaigning [...] The move to the right at a UK level by Labour confirmed that if a party was going to be progressive and stand up for Scotland then the SNP was the logical choice."

2015 General Election Result: SNP gain from Labour with a 25.3% majority.

28. Corrie Wilson
Constituency: Ayr, Carrick, and Cumnock
Year of Birth: Unknown

Quote: "The Referendum showed that there was a bunch of people out there who cared about their community, country, and fellow-citizens who wanted to make a better life. There were also people who did say 'well I'm alright, Jack, but there are people who are less fortunate and I would like to be part of making that change.'"

2015 General Election Result: SNP gain from Labour with a 21.6% majority.

29. Patricia Gibson

Constituency: North Ayrshire and Arran
Year of Birth: Unknown

Quote: "I believe that the only people who will make decisions in the best interest of Scotland are the Scottish people and they've mandated the SNP to do that, quite specifically in this election I think, and that's our job to make sure that we represent the values and interests and aspirations of the Scottish people."

2015 General Election Result: SNP gain from Labour with a 25.2% majority.

30. Phillippa Whitford

Constituency: Central Ayrshire
Year of Birth: 1959

Quote: "I had always believed in Scottish independence, but I had never joined a political party because if you are a voter you should put the party through their paces every single time. They should not be allowed to assume [that] they had your vote in your pocket. They should work for it."

2015 General Election Result: SNP gain from Labour with a 26.8% majority.

31. Stuart McDonald

Constituency: Cumbernauld, Kilsyth, and Kirkintilloch East
Year of Birth: 1978

Quote: "I'm sure people across the United Kingdom want to see a less unequal society [...] but people in other parts of the United Kingdom have repeatedly voted for centre right or right wing parties to achieve these things, whereas people in Scotland are continuing to vote for centre parties or centre left parties, so that's where I think the difference comes in. It's just a different political outlook."

2015 General Election Result: SNP gain from Labour with a 29.9% majority.

32. Marion Fellows
Constituency: Motherwell and Wishaw
Year of Birth: Unknown

Quote: "My political inspirations are varied: folk like Winnie Ewing, Margo MacDonald, and our present First Minister. I think I have always been most impressed by people who were in politics and believed what they were trying to do."

2015 General Election Result: SNP gain from Labour with a 24.7% majority.

33. Kirsten Oswald
Constituency: East Renfrewshire
Year of Birth: 1972

Quote: "People need to get a fair crack at the whip. It can't be all about the 1%, we need to think about the other 99%. Things are so diverse between the top and the bottom of society, and we need to normalise that."

2015 General Election Result: SNP gain from Labour with a 6.5% majority.

34. Angela Crawley
Constituency: Lanark and Hamilton East
Year of Birth: 1987

Quote: "We took our message beyond our sphere [in the 2015 General Election]. We weren't just talking to ourselves and we offered a positive message of hope to the people of Scotland."

2015 General Election Result: SNP gain from Labour with a 18.3% majority.

35. Phillip Boswell
Constituency: Coatbridge, Chryston and Bellshill
Year of Birth: 1963

Quote: I'm under no illusions: I'm part of a group of people who are doing politics for the right reasons. I don't know anybody yet who is in the mainframe style of politics and doing it for themselves. This is where my old party – the Labour Party – fall down badly and have done for quite some time."

2015 General Election Result: SNP gain from Labour with a 22.7% majority.

36. Neil Gray
Constituency: Airdrie and Shotts
Year of Birth: 1986

Quote: "I've always been interested in politics and current affairs. [...] My dad was a member of the local school board and fought a successful campaign with other parents to keep our wee school open and eventually get a new one built. That type of local community activism has stayed with me."

2015 General Election Result: SNP gain from Labour with a 19.8% majority.

37. John Nicolson
Constituency: East Dunbartonshire
Year of Birth: 1961

Quote: "I wanted to fight a positive [General Election campaign] that made people realise the benefit of voting SNP. What you want to do is inspire people with what politics can achieve."

2015 General Election Result: SNP gain from Liberal Democrats with a 4.0% majority.

38. John McNally
Constituency: Falkirk
Year of Birth: 1961

Quote: "The reason I became a councillor was because I wanted to change my local area. I've run my own hairdressing business for around forty years [...] I'm now just quite happy with a barber shop that I work in, which is the greatest way in the world to keep in communication with your local people."

2015 General Election Result: SNP gain from Independent with a 32.6% majority.

39. Martyn Day
Constituency: Linlithgow and East Falkirk
Year of Birth: 1971

Quote: "I will fight as hard as I possibly can for every single constituent in this constituency. It doesn't matter how they voted in the Referendum, it doesn't matter how they voted in [the General] election, I will fight tooth and nail for their interests."

2015 General Election Result: SNP gain from Labour with a 21.0% majority.

40. Lisa Cameron
Constituency: East Kilbride, Strathaven, and Lesmahagow
Year of Birth: 1972

Quote: "I was so impressed by Nicola Sturgeon throughout the Referendum. I think she has that unique ability to reach out the people and make them believe in politics again."

2015 General Election Result: SNP gain from Labour with a 27.3% majority.

41. Steven Paterson
Constituency: Stirling
Year of Birth: 1975

Quote: "In terms of the way Westminster works, it has some archaic and confusing conventions. However, it's like any other parliament: it's got its rules, there are ways to make them work for your advantage if you understand them; I've tried to make quick work of getting to know exactly how it works."

2015 General Election Result: SNP gain from Labour with a 20.1% majority.

42. Pete Wishart
Constituency: Perth and North Perthshire
Year of Birth: 1962

Quote: "One of the things I'm most proud about is that we [Runrig] introduced Gaelic to a new young generation of people who then saw its worth. We felt that we had control of a lost part of our history, which had almost been killed off by a number of UK or British interests."

2015 General Election Result: SNP hold with a 17.8% majority.

43. Tasmina Ahmed-Sheikh
Constituency: Ochil and South Perthshire
Year of Birth: 1970

Quote: "Something that has been noted by people down south in the House of Commons is that Scotland has a very [politically] engaged population, and many politicians from different political parties often say that they wished it was the same where they were canvassing."

2015 General Election Result: SNP gain from Labour with a 17.6% majority.

44. Douglas Chapman
Constituency: Dunfermline and West Fife
Year of Birth: 1955

Quote: "We [in Scotland] have huge issues with the health of the nation and levels of poverty, especially amongst young children. These have been the driving factors for me throughout my whole political career. If we can create the kind of country where everyone has a fair chance then that is the overall goal."

2015 General Election Result: SNP gain from Labour with a 18.5% majority.

45. Stephen Gethins
Constituency: North East Fife
Year of Birth: 1976

Quote: "I felt very at home politically in the SNP [when I joined aged seventeen]. What always drove me was the international outlook. I always thought the real isolation was the Union, and it frustrated me that you had to deal with the rest of the world through the prism of London."

2015 General Election Result: SNP gain from Liberal Democrats with a 9.6% majority.

46. Peter Grant
Constituency: Glenrothes
Year of Birth: 1961

Quote: "The way the [General Election 2015] campaign team pulled itself together was like nothing I've ever seen before. We really did have people from all walks of life, all wanting to be heard."

2015 General Election Result: SNP gain from Labour with a 29.2% majority.

47. Roger Mullin
Constituency: Kircaldy and Cowdenbeath
Year of Birth: 1948

Quote: "[My parents] were very caring about the community. My dad always had this mantra, he said that everybody in this world is good at something. In that sense he not only cared but admired the potential of people, and would have wanted to see everybody having the opportunity to flourish."

2015 General Election Result: SNP gain from Labour with a 18.9% majority.

48. Hannah Bardell
Constituency: Livingston
Year of Birth: 1984

Quote: "[...] people are so disengaged with the 'same old, same old' of politics. You can only give people second class political representation for so long, and I think before that [...] we hadn't engaged people yet. When we did, and we gave them uniquely Scottish answers to uniquely Scottish questions, that started to resonate."

2015 General Election Result: SNP gain from Labour with a 29.3% majority.

49. George Kerevan
Constituency: East Lothian
Year of Birth: 1949

Quote: "Piecemeal devolution – granting a concession here and a concession there, a change here and a change there –

has hardly resolved the issue of the Scottish desire for self-government."

2015 General Election Result: SNP gain from Labour with a 11.5% majority.

50. Owen Thompson
Constituency: Midlothian
Year of Birth: 1978

Quote: "I think the election of the 56 is the people of Scotland very loudly saying that they rejected the Tory austerity agenda. The [issue of] independence is still very separate to a lot of people. We've still got a case to make and ultimately I think the Scottish people will tell us when they're ready for it."

2015 General Election Result: SNP gain from Labour with a 20.4% majority.

51. Deidre Brock
Constituency: Edinburgh North and Leith
Year of Birth: 1961

Quote: "I see so many examples of small successful European countries without oil, but with people with grit and determination like Scotland. I think the SNP government has shown the way, even with limited powers at its command in running the country. I believe utterly in the strengths and abilities of the Scottish people."

2015 General Election Result: SNP gain from Labour with a 9.7% majority.

52. Joanna Cherry QC
Constituency: Edinburgh South West
Year of Birth: 1966

Quote: "I'd like to see us model ourselves on the modern South African constitution and their constitutional court: a wonderful constitution that encompasses social and economic rights as well as basic human rights. Also, I would like Scotland to be a constitutional democracy with a president rather that a monarch."

2015 General Election Result: SNP gain from Labour with a 15.8% majority.

53. Michelle Thomson
Constituency: Edinburgh West
Year of Birth: Unknown

Quote: "[...] if someone says 'black is black is black' I will always say 'white' and likewise the other way around. I don't necessarily always argue against things in public, especially now I'm a politician, but I always ask: why do you want me to think that? I like being contrary, and it's healthy to always think of the alternative."

2015 General Election Result: SNP gain from Liberal Democrats with a 5.8% majority.

54. Tommy Sheppard
Constituency: Edinburgh East
Year of Birth: 1959

Quote: "The reason why I'm in the SNP is because I became convinced during the noughties of the case for independence and that independence was a way of achieving the type of democratic social reforms that I'd always believed in and still believe in."

2015 General Election Result: SNP gain from Labour with a 19.3% majority.

55. Richard Arkless
Constituency: Dumfries and Galloway
Year of Birth: 1975

Quote: "I would describe myself as a social democrat in that I passionately believe in social justice. That's not to say that we're totally different from the rest of the UK but for me it's the interaction between social justice and a growing economy that makes a true social democrat and coming from an economic background that was always my interest."

2015 General Election Result: SNP gain from Labour with a 11.5% majority.

56. Calum Kerr
Constituency: Berwickshire, Roxburgh and Selkirk
Year of Birth: 1972

Quote: "The day after the Referendum I was an emotional wreck. Lots of people were texting me saying how proud they were, and on came the tears. I had a day of that and then I said we are not giving up."

2015 General Election Result: SNP gain from Liberal Democrats with a 0.6% majority.

About The Author

Iain Macwhirter is an award-winning political commentator for the *Sunday Herald* and *The Herald*. Iain started at the BBC as a researcher after graduating from Edinburgh University, and became the BBC's Scottish Political Correspondent in 1987. In 1990 he moved to London to present political programmes for BBC network television such as 'Westminster Live' and 'Scrutiny'. He was a member of the Westminster Lobby for nearly ten years and columnist for a number of national newspapers including *The Observer* and *The Scotsman*. In 1999 he returned to Scotland to help launch the *Sunday Herald* and to present the BBC's 'Holyrood Live' TV programmes. He was also Rector of Edinburgh University 2009-11. In a co-production with STV in 2013, Iain presented a three-part history of Scottish Nationalism, *Road to Referendum. Disunited Kingdom* (2014) was his second book, following *Road to Referendum* (2013).

Acknowledgements

The author would like to thank Gill Tasker, Helen Sedgwick, Simon Cree, and Mark Buckland of Cargo Publishing.

Praise for Disunited Kingdom

'An involving and thoughtful survey of a late spring in Scotland's political and cultural life.' – Stephen Daisley, STV

'Cerebral and thought-provoking... Iain Macwhirter makes his argument powerfully.' – Andrew Sparrow, The *Guardian*

'His writing and broadcasting on politics in Scotland have been the benchmark by which many of us judge our own, more modest, contributions.' – Kevin McKenna, The *Observer*

'An authoritative and peerless sequel to Road to Referendum.' – The *List*

'Whenever the next referendum arrives people will look to *Disunited Kingdom* for a succinct and eloquent analysis of what happened the first time.' – *Scottish Review of Books*

'Might just be the definitive account of the #indyref experience. Ace.' – Alan Bissett, Author & Playwright

'A corker... an excellent first draft of history.' – David Greig, Playwright